More Praise for *Ultimate Relianc*

"Thank you, Sue! This is just the resource that is needed for ... and churches who desire the discovery and leading of God's Spirit. The Breakthrough stories are inspirational and motivating. The 'prayer-hold' practices are thoughtful and help individuals and teams dive deeper into the great well of prayer."

—Tim Craig, senior pastor, Great Bridge United Methodist Church, Chesapeake, VA

"Sue Nilson Kibbey is a much-needed leader for the twenty-first-century church. The current climate and culture create a challenging landscape for us as we seek to advance Christ's mission and share the gospel. Too many times, we think that the burden is on us to construct new and innovative approaches. We forget that if we do not first embrace dependence on the One who called us, we will continue to spin our proverbial wheels. In *Ultimate Reliance,* Sue gives us a methodology for staying connected to our true power source!"

—Chip Freed, lead pastor, Garfield Memorial Church, Cleveland, OH; national coach, Mosaix Global Network

"Ultimate Reliance: Breakthrough Prayer Practices for Leaders reminds us of the simple beauty and power of prayer. It teaches biblically sound principles and effective, instructional exercises. It celebrates prayer. This book will deepen and enliven the dynamism embodied in persistent and expectant conversations with God."

—F. Willis Johnson, United Methodist elder, West Ohio Conference; author, *Holding Up Your Corner: Talking about Race in Your Community*, from Abingdon Press

"Sue Nilsen Kibbey has years of practical experience helping pastors and congregations experience spiritual renewal through praying brief, heartfelt prayers for God's guidance. Her vivid illustrations in this book of how God has answered the persistent prayers of individuals and groups in miraculous ways are encouraging to those who have run dry 'doing it on their own.' If you want God to renew your life personally and your congregation to experience the living presence of God in the world, then read, study, and put into action the five Breakthrough Prayer Practices, which have led hundreds of congregations to become spiritually renewed and actively engaged in God's mission in the world."

—Kent Millard, president, United Theological Seminary, Dayton, OH

Additional Books by the Author

Flood Gates: Holy Momentum for a Fearless Church

*Ultimately Responsible: When You're in Charge
of Igniting a Ministry*

Transformation Journal: A Daily Walk in the Word
(with Carolyn Slaughter and Kevin Applegate)

*Transformation Journal: A One Year Journey Through
the Bible* (with Carolyn Slaughter)

Find additional information and resources at
snkibbey.com and ultimate-reliance.com.

**To purchase introductory videos for each
chapter of *Ultimate Reliance*,
please visit:**

www.cokesbury.com/ultimate-reliance-study

SUE NILSON KIBBEY

ULTIMATE
RELIANCE

BREAKTHROUGH PRAYER PRACTICES FOR LEADERS

Abingdon Press™

Nashville

ULTIMATE RELIANCE:
BREAKTHROUGH PRAYER PRACTICES FOR LEADERS
Copyright © 2019 by Sue Nilson Kibbey

This book is printed on acid-free paper.

Library of Congress Cataloging-in-Publication Data has been requested.

ISBN: 978-1-5018-7093-4

Scripture quotations marked CEB are taken from the Common English Bible. Copyright © 2011 by the Common English Bible. All rights reserved. Used by permission. www.CommonEnglishBible.com.

Scripture quotations marked NASB are taken from the New American Standard Bible® (NASB), Copyright © 1960, 1962, 1963, 1968, 1971, 1973, 1975, 1977, 1995 by The Lockman Foundation. Used by permission. www.Lockman.org

Scripture quotations marked NLT are taken from the Holy Bible, New Living Translation, copyright © 1996, 2004, 2015 by Tyndale House Foundation. Used by permission of Tyndale House Publishers, Inc., Carol Stream, Illinois 60188. All rights reserved.

19 20 21 22 23 24 25 26 27 28—10 9 8 7 6 5 4 3 2 1
MANUFACTURED IN THE UNITED STATES OF AMERICA

I'm grateful...

for what I've learned from Pastor Caleb and his congregation
     of fearless, selfless followers of Jesus
     as they navigate the whitewaters of spiritual adventure—
     ultimately reliant on the power of breakthrough prayer

for Joseph, John and Michelle, Dan, Sarai, Kabamba
     and Forest Chapel Church,
     whose breakthrough prayer video stories introduce each chapter—
     also for videographer Michael Pollard's extraordinary
     "digital storytelling" talent

and for the countless clergy, leaders, and congregations everywhere
     who have already embraced and deployed
     Breakthrough Prayer Initiatives
     that are unleashing the movement of Jesus, the Church,
     with renewed hope and possibilities

CONTENTS

Begin Here

MAXIMIZING YOUR PRAYER MOMENTUM WITH THIS RESOURCE

God is the
One Great Circumstance.

Since the publication of *Flood Gates: Holy Momentum for a Fearless Church* (2016, Abingdon Press) together with Breakthrough Prayer Initiative training events I have led for pastors and church teams across the country, a growing groundswell of prayers for new God dreams and possibilities to break through in congregations of every conceivable size and setting has continued to rise and spread.

The invitation and encouragement to include the simple additive prayer component of also asking God for—along with healing, strength, protection, comfort, and wisdom—new breakthroughs of opportunities and potentialities to show up and show out is what a "breakthrough prayer initiative" is all about. And when a congregation both individually and collectively adds this ongoing, across all ages and in all settings from worship to meetings to classes to choir rehearsals to youth group gatherings and even the children's classes, it's clear that hearts are swung wide open spiritually. and that God loves to answer.

In fact, if your church or ministry is discouraged and seems stuck in the habit of perennially looking "down and in" with discouragement, the additive component of asking God in your mutual prayer life for new breakthrough possibilities to unfold is the most powerful and effective catalyst I've ever seen. It has the miraculous potential to shift your collective gaze "up and out" instead, finally seeing and anticipating where God wants to lead you next. It can transform a "woe is us" church refrain to "wow, look at us!"—assuming of course, that when you pray, **you genuinely believe that prayer makes a difference**.

You see, it's entirely possible for a congregation, for its leaders, and for you personally to have only an intellectual belief in the importance and value of prayer. Prayer might open and close meetings in your setting, for example, including naming prayer concerns by those in attendance or asking God to bless ministry efforts already underway. Your weekly worship service typically includes prayer—perhaps led by the pastor or read collectively from your hymnal, worship bulletin, or liturgical guidebook. The Lord's Prayer is a sacred, historic ritual repeated together in most churches. And you yourself likely have a prayer life, however informal and sporadic at times it may feel, where you ask God for help, calm, protection, safekeeping, healing for loved ones or you, and provision of a need you may have or see in the moment.

But once any of those prayers have been offered, do you really believe without question that there will be a Spirit-fueled response starting to unfold immediately on a divine timeframe, activated by the loving Almighty who is listening?

How easy it is, unfortunately, for a person, leadership team, or congregation to pray—and then proceed from there with the reverse low-expectation attitude that your prayer faces the unlikeliness that God will actually act. In fact, those with only an intellectual belief about prayer may not even actively look, observe, or notice how and when God's response starts breaking through. When you have merely an intellectual belief in prayer, you may even conclude that God doesn't often answer *just because God hasn't followed your exact instructions when you prayed*. So your expectations about the efficacy of prayer remain low.

Here's the difference between simply having a belief that prayer is important, versus committing all of who you are—your heart, mind, spirit, and will—to the thoroughgoing, expectational conviction that *prayer does make a difference*.

It's completely releasing the assumption that God's supernatural, all-encompassing transformational love should only manifest the way you want it to, when you request that it should. It's instead surrendering to the profound, game-changing reality that God's all-loving response to your prayers will be in accordance to a far greater miraculous Hand, fueled with redemptive intention beyond what you could ask, think, or imagine. And so when we pray, we can ask God as specifically as we want or for what we believe would be best—and in so doing, trust that God's response will be even better or different according to a renewing, reconciling, resurrection-infused redemptive wisdom far beyond ours.

Are you willing to embrace your prayer life, and the prayers of your team and congregation, as "spiritual electricity" of a nature that cannot always be anticipated but carries that kind of supernatural power and energy directed by God's Spirit? If you choose to make this your unshakeable bedrock understanding of prayer, even when you have moments or seasons of human doubt or impatience, you will find yourself—and your church—living into your prayers with no-holds-barred openness. You will lean toward, grow observant of, and remain surrendered to God's responses. And it will be the path to exciting and challenging spiritual adventures beyond your imagination in your own maturing faith, in your life as a leader, in your congregation, and in God's ability to use you as a world-changer for Christ.

Why the Title *Ultimate Reliance* and the River-Rapids Photo on This Book's Cover?

If you've read *Flood Gates: Holy Momentum for a Fearless Church*, you'll already know what it means when I describe a conversation with Pastor Caleb, one that took place earlier this year, as a "Conflux Moment."

If you're not yet familiar with that term, let me explain. A Conflux Moment is what I call one of those occasions in which you unmistakably realize that the Holy Spirit and your own human spirit are synchronistically making contact. In that human-divine moment of confluence is birthed a new glimpse of spiritual clarity and inspiration, along with a push of momentum forward. Some also refer to this as a "Holy Spirit moment" or a "breakthrough moment."

Pastor Caleb was updating me on the revitalization progress unfolding in his church via the resourcing/training that had been provided by the Missional Church Consultation Initiative (MCCI) that I lead. He explained that his leadership board had read and discussed *Flood Gates* together one chapter at a time over the last several months. After the second chapter of *Flood Gates* that describes the fundamentals of how to orchestrate a Breakthrough Prayer Initiative, Caleb and his board were beginning every monthly meeting with a prayer walk through all of the spaces in their facility and asking God to do the amazing and impossible in and through church ministries, service, and outreach. And Caleb added that he himself, as their leader, had read and reread my earlier church leadership book, *Ultimately Responsible* (2006, Abingdon Press), seeking to fulfill everything God has called him to be in his role.

Then Caleb made the statement that God's Spirit transformed into a Conflux Moment for me.

"You know, I've realized a couple of things in all this. One is that if you are going to lead your team to pray for new and ongoing God possibilities, dreams, and breakthroughs, you better be prepared for the spiritual adventure of your life—because *all of you praying this way together begins to feel like you're amateurs who are raft-riding the rapids of 'Holy Spirit waters' that are gushing out of open floodgates, and you're all hanging on for dear life.* Nothing happens the way you planned it when you pray that kind of prayer. The church becomes a literal movement surging forward!

"And the other thing I've realized is that, for a leader, the only way to succeed at being 'ultimately responsible' like your earlier leadership book's title is to first learn in your own prayer life how to be **ultimately reliant** on God yourself. I keep telling my board that without their—and my own—personal breakthrough prayer practices, it's impossible to demonstrate the spiritual courage and faith to navigate the river of breakthroughs unleashed by this kind of prayer. And that our personal breakthrough prayer practices are what will inspire the entire membership to do the same."

Why This Resource?

As the Breakthrough Prayer Initiative has spread, an overwhelming number of pastors and church members have reached out and asked for a resource that will continue to fuel their congregation's prayer momentum. They have also asked how to help church leaders mature and grow—to develop a deep "ultimate reliance" on God—as they live into the practice of a breakthrough prayer habit both collectively and individually. To really believe that prayer makes a difference at the heart level. Are you hungry to add the simple breakthrough prayer practice into every aspect of your daily life? Are you ready to learn how your church leadership team, committee, class, or ministry can incorporate breakthrough prayer practices as, united, you navigate the rapids of God's Spirit in your shared work and service? If so, this resource is for you.

What Are "Breakthrough Prayer Practices"?

A breakthrough prayer initiative is a movement in which an entire congregation, the body of Christ, begins feasting on prayer as its spiritual food for vitality, energy, and strength. It is a *movement* rather than just a prayer class series, new program, or sermon series preached annually. A breakthrough prayer initiative doesn't replace the existing prayer life of your congregation. Rather, it is an additive component. In addition to prayers for healing, hope, courage, wisdom, and comfort, a breakthrough prayer initiative adds a request in every prayer occasion for God to break through with new possibilities, hopes and dreams without limits—both in the life of our church, and in our own lives…and that we surrender ourselves to what God may unfold.

> If you haven't yet launched a foundational breakthrough prayer initiative like this at your church, that's the very first step I recommend. Be sure to check out the second chapter of *Flood Gates*, where I've already provided instructions, stories, and examples as assistance to get you started on how to create and establish a churchwide breakthrough prayer initiative. It's the best initial way to get started with shifting prayer to the center of everything.

In the pages to come here, **breakthrough prayer practices** are defined as specific one-sentence (or even one-word) prayers that are loaded with spiritual dynamite, asking God to break through in a particular aspect. They are for you as a ministry leader, along with those around you, to begin to more potently equip your own prayer lives on a daily basis both individually and together as your breakthrough prayer initiative moves forward.

My intent is to provide a chapter-by-chapter guide for learning, discussing, and applying, one by one, simple breakthrough prayer practices that will then become powerful spiritual habits the Holy Spirit will use to enable you and your spiritual traveling companions to intentionally live and lead with ultimate reliance on God. It may also assist in renewing and refueling, again and again, the foundational surge of a breakthrough prayer movement coursing through the spiritual veins of your entire congregation through use by groups, ministries, committees, and classes who dare to embrace specific breakthrough prayer practices.

And—if you are reading this right now and your breakthrough prayer life is a solo journey, *Ultimate Reliance* is definitely for you as well.

Here's what you can expect from *Ultimate Reliance.*

Each chapter provides:

- a **short introductory video story** by a ministry leader or leaders on the chapter's theme to view when your team, class, or group gathers (or as you move through this resource individually) that will set the stage for your discussion and application or journaling (these videos are available for purchase at www.cokesbury.com/ultimate-reliance-study)

- an overarching, powerful scripture-based **one-sentence breakthrough prayer practice**, plus promptings on how to customize your own—even one-word prayers

- **biblical** context and learning

- **stories** of actual leaders or congregations who utilized this particular breakthrough prayer practice (all are true stories, with names and details changed for privacy)

- **application and discussion or journaling questions** both for you individually, and for your leadership team, class or group collectively

- a **quick summary** of each breakthrough prayer practice

As you move through *Ultimate Reliance* chapter by chapter, you'll find yourself internalizing the set of one-sentence breakthrough prayer practices that by regular use will become woven into the fabric of your faith, heart, and spirit. You will notice growing readiness in yourself, as well as together with others around you, to identify one or another of the breakthrough prayer practices to select when needed for a unique moment, challenge, or circumstance, and to pray it as often as it arises.

You can learn to let these short breakthrough prayer practices accompany you always, and allow them to move you again and again into spiritual surrender and expectancy for how your prayers will indeed serve as an invitation to God's breakthrough hopes, dreams, and potential for Jesus. You may even find yourself gradually adding some of your own unique one-sentence breakthrough prayers to this book's collection that help will equip and keep you vital and growing in your prayer life, opening the door to God's divine activity and response in every moment.

To Start: What's Needed to Develop Breakthrough Prayer Practices as a Leader

As you may understand by now, *Ultimate Reliance* is not intended for inspirational reading only. It's to help you learn practically to apply your core burning conviction that prayer, indeed, makes a difference to your life of faith. Breakthrough prayer allows the Holy Spirit to seep, flow, or surge through your reservations, discouragement, questions, and dead ends—and you will look up and out in hope as you invite God's response of metamorphic, supernatural love to transform and prevail.

So gird the following scriptural assurances firmly around your spiritual self as we now set out together through the following pages.

- Accept God's peace through faith-filled confidence *that the moment we pray, a divine response is underway and unfolding* according to God's preferred timeline and handiwork. (Matthew 7:11)

- Cultivate an attitude of open expectancy. God's responses to your breakthrough prayers are likely to be *different or better than that for which you have asked*, and in a *timeframe* that may be different than what you assume. (Luke 11:11-13)

- Be confident that *God is able to do far more* than we could ask or imagine. (Ephesians 3:20)

- Remember that in Christ, *we are already provided with everything* pertaining to life and godliness. (2 Peter 1:3)

- Embrace fully that *nothing can separate us* from the love of Christ. (Romans 8:38-39)

An Image to Carry with You...

For my own breakthrough prayer practices, I carry with me a small single strand with five colored beads. Each bead reminds me of one single-sentence breakthrough prayer, and all of them together have become a spiritually stabilizing prayer framework I've internalized that has equipped me to be ready prayer-wise in the unique moments that comprise a day—whether surprises, crises, challenges, opportunities. At the start of every morning, I pray through them all. Then any of these breakthrough prayers are refreshed and ready to be prayed again as the situation or need arises through the unfolding of the day. I sometimes notice myself asking myself, "Which breakthrough prayer do I need right now?" and in my mind's eye, I quickly sort through the breakthrough prayer beads on the strand until the Spirit helps identify which to pray. Often, one of them pops up in my spirit unsolicited on its own.

So in the chapters that follow, let me introduce you to these five breakthrough prayer practices, one by one. I acknowledge that the chapters to come have been written with the "pen" of my own life of prayer. I am honored that we are companions in the adventure of breakthrough prayer—and I am praying for you in your pursuit to move prayer to the central practice of your earthly life of faith. If you haven't yet launched a foundational breakthrough prayer initiative like this at your church, that's the very first step I recommend. Be sure to check out the second chapter of *Flood Gates,* where I've already provided instructions, stories and examples as assistance to get you started on how to create and establish a churchwide breakthrough prayer initiative. It's the best initial way to get started with shifting prayer to the center of everything. May you let go of any limiting beliefs so that you, your team, and your church may experience, without any limits, what God can do.

Oswald Chambers, great Scottish devotional leader of the last century, has been a longtime spiritual mentor of mine through his writings. Let's move forward together upon a few words of his advice—which validate for us where "ultimate reliance" truly begins.

We pray
when there's nothing else
we can do—
but God wants us to pray
before we do anything at all.

"UPSURGE"
BREAKTHROUGH PRAYER

Hear my cry, O God;
Give heed to my prayer.
From the end of the earth I call to You when my heart is faint;
Lead me to the rock that is higher than I.

—Psalm 61:1-2 (NASB)

WATCH #1 Video Breakthrough Prayer Practice Story: Joseph

Find introductory videos featuring true stories that illustrate the
breakthrough prayer practice for each chapter of *Ultimate Reliance* at:
www.cokesbury.com/ultimate-reliance-study

It was the soul-level moment out of which a heartfelt cry to God emerges. The psalmist David was in a dilemma. History suggests he might have had enemies in hot pursuit. Or maybe he had taken a path through the hills that he believed would cut an hour off his travel time to the destination, never dreaming of the humanly impassible crags that lay ahead. It could have been he was hoping to gain a strategic view, ensure himself additional safety, or reach a perch of spiritual significance by choosing that particular route. Or it's plausible he assumed he would meet up with helpful traveling companions along that passage. Likely he had strong confidence in his own agile expertise that had always gotten him where he wanted to go, no matter how forbidding the cliffs.

But along the climb he reached a spot at which he recognized to push farther was going to require much more than his remaining reserves. His heart, or in scripture's original Hebrew language, sometimes translated as his "seat of courage," was faint within him. Physical exhaustion was likely. His hiking equipment was inadequate for what he faced. Yet David courageously hung on to his resolve for the destination that beckoned him.

It was then he prayed what I call an Upsurge Prayer, a simple breakthrough prayer asking God to "Lead me to the rock that is higher than I...."

David's prayer contained an intentional choice of words. The Hebrew word for "lead" is also used by Old Testament writers elsewhere in scripture to describe a shepherd guiding a flock. It's the same word that Moses used to depict how the pillar of smoke by day and fire by night led the children of Israel through the wilderness (Exodus 13:21). So David, in this moment of prayer, was asking for miraculous spiritual guidance and resourcing to break through from God—whether through shepherd-like nudges or with brilliant supernatural drama. Lead me....

Note also that David's Hebrew phrasing in his prayer that's translated "higher than I" means literally "to lift up." It was Hebrew language wording more typically used to characterize what parents do when they are raising children, rearing their young to grow up into maturity and adulthood.

So wrapped in the Upsurge Breakthrough Prayer from David was a courageous request to

shepherd me, resource me...
with the same supernatural directive that you provided in the pillar of
*   smoke and fire,*
the same firm, gentle hand of a shepherd,
the same loving, strong hand of a heavenly Parent,
to lift me up to the next place that only you can help me reach.

Grow me up—beyond my current capacity, capability, and maturity—to
realize the rock that is higher than I.

The Spiritual Path: An Invitation to Ascend

How would you define the phrase "spiritual path," or often called "discipleship pathway"? In some congregations, "discipleship" is the name of the list of Sunday classes that are offered each quarter. You may have heard it as part of the job title of a paid staff person, such as

Director of Discipleship, where the title is intended to indicate that the role carries responsibility to set up spiritual growth opportunities for the congregation. "Commitment to discipleship" might be included in the vows a new church member takes to indicate Christian faith.

Discipleship—or the spiritual path of faith—is actually the mechanism through which God brings a maturing of the Christ life inside you, and a subsequent transformation of who you are into Christ's likeness. It doesn't happen only through a weekly "discipleship class" you take. Fact is, your spiritual path is far wider, and includes all of earthly life as your spiritual "classroom." Any opportunity, challenge, roadblock, detour, triumph, or tragedy that come along are all potential discipling scenarios within which God longs to beckon you to grasp the divine hand in trust and dare to progress spiritually beyond where you could go on your own.

The earthly spiritual path's ascent, should you agree to take it, results in "growing you up" so that you develop the new life of Christ inside that's expressed by an unmistakable likeness of Jesus on the outside. How will you know it's happening? The confirmation in you will be evident through emergence of Fruit of the Spirit: love, joy, peace, patience, kindness, goodness, faithfulness, gentleness, and self-control (Galatians 5:22-23 CEB). And God's perspective that you'll gain from the rock that is higher than you will provide confirmation through and through that the climb, whatever the cost, is always worth more than you could have imagined.

Cost? Yes, growing up into Christ's likeness requires the leaving behind of what you might have always previously felt were non-negotiables. "Climbing equipment" (habitual ways of thinking or behaving) that you found useful in the past and the "baggage" of deep-seated attitudes, pride, or insecurities of heart and mind must be released in order to miraculously reach the next handhold. And maybe you've noticed that there are countless comfortable park benches alongside your spiritual path that make it entirely too easy to decide to sit down and just take in the partial view from there (and keep hanging on to the baggage). That's far easier than surrendering to the cost—the transformations you'll have to undergo—of scaling the summit.

You understand, now, that the Upsurge Breakthrough Prayer practice on your spiritual path is not a request for safety or protection. It's like the "Archer Prayer" style I described in chapter 2 of my book *Flood*

Gates, breakthrough prayer that aims specifically at your longing for God to mature you further, whatever it takes.

Lead Me to the Rock That Is Higher Than I: Ministry Leadership

I remember a close friend in a Bible study group who was known for her wonderful personality. Alicia lit up the room when she entered. She was always the first to get everyone laughing, was always the catalyst to spark discussion. The atmosphere was noticeably lacking at the Bible study if, for some reason, Alicia couldn't attend that night.

Alicia always talked in our group about her love for Christ and of her confidence that God would eventually lead her to a way she could serve at our church most effectively. So we were all excited when Alicia told us one evening that she had been invited to become the hospitality team's front door greeter on Sunday mornings. What a perfect match for Alicia's overflowing enthusiasm toward life and people!

Alicia fulfilled her Sunday morning greeter role for several months, regaling our Bible study with stories of newcomers she had welcomed and the fun she had serving with others on the hospitality team. Then one week, Alicia asked us to pray with her about a new invitation she had received. The longtime hospitality team leader had announced she would be stepping aside and had asked if Alicia would like to take on the responsibility.

Alicia explained her decision-making considerations. "Truthfully, I have found myself becoming a little unhappy and dissatisfied every Sunday when I arrive to serve in my usual greeter role because I can't help but notice the person who has been the team leader. I feel I can take responsibility for the team more cheerfully than she has been demonstrating. I have also wondered what she has actually been doing for the team besides sending out a serving schedule each month. Making and sending out a schedule? That's something I know I could do, and I'm also pretty cheerful by nature—definitely more than her. So this seems like a great potential next step.

"I feel certain that God will bless me with even more peace and joy as I lead the entire hospitality team to welcome newcomers. Plus, it will be perceived as a position of respect in our congregation, a sign to others that I am viewed by the nominations committee as spiritually mature enough to move further into leadership. I feel thrilled to accept."

With the full support of the Bible study group, Alicia excitedly took leadership of the team. At first she smiled whenever the group asked her how the new role was going and said, "Great!" But as weeks passed, her smile lessened and, uncharacteristically, her comments and interaction during the study and discussion time declined.

Then one week Alicia arrived to Bible study, looking visibly upset. Emotional words began pouring out.

"I thought becoming the hospitality team leader would be a wonderful time. But here's the thing. The total opposite has happened. There's no joy, no fun. This job is impossible!

"There are several big issues. Some of the hospitality team members don't show up regularly on their assigned Sunday mornings even after I've sent out a serving schedule, and they don't let me know ahead of time. So I am continually frustrated and have no idea how to inspire them and get them to understand the importance of what we are there to do. I get discouraged and have had my feelings hurt by their behavior. I believe I have every right to expect respect and support as their team leader, but instead it seems like they now socialize with each other more than with me, and I haven't figured out why. It feels so unkind. No one asks if they can give me a hand with anything extra, and it doesn't help that I've never been comfortable inviting people to help me. But they should just want to do that, shouldn't they? Bottom line, I have to stay much longer than everyone else after the worship service has ended in order to organize and put away our team's supplies myself.

"It is demanding much more of my personal time than I ever anticipated. It feels like God has abandoned me and all I have are irritations and hindrances, trying to get my arms around what I am doing. I feel like a failure and want out of this leadership role. I have a picture in my mind of an amazing, over-the-top atmosphere of love and welcome our team could someday achieve. But how can I do my job as the team leader when the team doesn't do what they are supposed to do? How am I supposed to know how to get them to be committed? I want to go back to being the sanctuary front door greeter. I know how to do that. With the team leadership, I am way out of my comfort zone and I don't like it at all."

Perhaps as you are reading this true story, the Upsurge Breakthrough Prayer practice of David is resonating inside your spirit. You may be wondering if Alicia as a ministry leader was at the same analogous spiritual point as David had been in his physical rocky ascent. I can almost hear you pointing out that she was considering choosing an easy, comfortable seat along the side of her spiritual path, rather than praying for God's supernatural resources to equip her onward to the summit visible with the eyes of her heart.

Back to the Bible study that night. All of us looked at each other. Then one person began.

"Alicia, we are all so sorry to hear this has presented an unexpected scenario for you. Once you look past your initial disillusionment with the role, which is so different than what you anticipated it would be, what specifically challenges you the most?"

Alicia reflected. "Well, like I said, the first thing is that I have no idea how to inspire the hospitality team to show up and serve on their assigned shifts. That always seemed to happen like clockwork before, back while I was just a member of the team. But now that I'm the team leader, it seems hit and miss. I don't know what to do, and quite frankly I just don't want to keep hitting my head against that wall."

Someone else tried a different question. "Have you met with the previous hospitality team leader and asked her for wisdom and advice from her long season of leading the team? It sounds like from what you just said that she had figured out how to do that."

Alicia's gaze dropped, and she paused. "Well, I didn't have a conversation like that with her when I started because I thought I probably had better ideas than she did. And if I asked her to meet now and share advice after I've already had my first couple of months in this role, I would lose face. It would be too embarrassing. It might be humiliating. I'm not going to admit to her I am struggling. I would really have to swallow my pride, and I hate doing that."

"So you would rather hang on to your pride, instead of casting it aside in exchange for practical guidance that could enable you to be effective at doing what God has called you to do?" another friend in the group prodded.

Again, silence. Then Alicia continued. "I just don't like how most of the hospitality team members no longer chat with me and are friendlier with each other. It feels hurtful. It didn't used to be that way before

I became the team leader. But at the same time, my opinion of the persons on the team has dropped significantly with their irresponsibility to show up as scheduled. They are clearly not very mature Christians."

The group kept pressing her. "Do you suppose your judgmental view of them is what has diminished their warmth toward you? Maybe they can sense your critical attitude. What would happen if you let go of judging them and sincerely loved and accepted each one just as they are, whether they always show up or not?"

"I can't do that," she shot back. "They might think their behavior is acceptable, and it is not. Besides, they never offer to help me with anything. I didn't know that there was so much to do at the end of every Sunday morning to put away hospitality supplies and keep things in order. And don't bother to suggest that I ask them to stay and help. I get feelings of self-inadequacy if I have to ask someone to give me a hand. I know in my head that's not the case, but please don't say I need to change my thinking about that. It's been part of my frame of mind since childhood, and it would be very difficult to give in and change after all these years.

"So, as you can see, I'm just not cut out for this team leader role. Okay, when it comes right down to it, I guess I don't like getting pushed to change and grow. It's much more comfortable to be the way I am, even if I do have some judgmentalism in me and prefer to avoid appearing incompetent by asking for help or advice. God created me just the way I am, I guess. I am not even going to pray about this. I am just going to tell the church nominations committee that I want to go back to front door greeting. That's enough for me."

You might argue, after listening in on this story thus far, that Alicia had a right to be disappointed that her obedience to God's prompting to embrace a new, more significant leadership role did not initially result in satisfaction and joy.

But do you suppose that, more importantly, Alicia had actually stumbled across a truth about the spiritual path of a leader? The expedition of genuine discipleship includes seasons of precipitation, heavy at times, of the unanticipated, unforeseen, and unpredictable. Although on the path we do also find ourselves led through vistas of green pastures or beside beautiful, still waters, the spiritual path's purpose is not accomplished by offering only unbroken coziness with guaranteed and contented safety.

If you ever felt frustrations similar to Alicia's as you have attempted to lead others, you may have already discovered your own version of David's Upsurge Prayer practice, a breakthrough request for God to help you reach farther into the impossible to fulfill God's purpose. And, like Alicia did, you also had to surrender some baggage to enhance your spiritual adroitness for the challenge.

"Alicia, listen. Do you really, really want to miss all the benefits God could bring you through the growth process of learning to lead? Stop and think about it. What if you prayed to be willing to surrender your pride (which doesn't honor God in any way, shape, or form) and schedule coffee with the former team leader to ask her how she kept the team so inspired and committed? Just imagine what you could learn that would help you both now and in the future as a leader."

"Yes!" said another Bible study member. "And what would it take for you to love and care about each hospitality team member as beloved children of God above anything else? And what if you took the initiative to find out about their families and their work like you used to, and to pray for each of them? Do you suppose God cares more about you loving them as people than drawing critical conclusions about them?"

Alicia began to cry. "Now, don't tell me I have to learn to ask people for help. I just can't do that. I feel self-value when I can do things myself, even though I am capable of resenting others for not pitching in. That is so much part of my identity, I just cannot let that go. I won't."

I remember our Bible study leader reaching over and giving her a gentle hug. That kind, wordless gesture seemed to bolster Alicia's courage. "So you all think we could pray together tonight and ask God to give me a miraculous spiritual breakthrough to live into a new version of me—one who can finally let go of what is holding me back? I feel terrified, and yet also hungry for it. Thirsty for it. I can't do this on my own. Oh God, grow me up and into more and more of you!"

Lead me to the Rock that is higher than I. . . .

What Can Distract an Upsurge Prayer Focus?

Many ministry leaders have told me that they long to fulfill a larger and more kingdom-shaping unique purpose through their lives as Jesus followers, but despite their best intentions they find themselves side-lined. What are common distractions to embracing fully an Upsurge Prayer practice?

One is the counterproductive habit of **complaining.** Complaining about the challenge, what it will require, or that God expects you to trust more or extend yourself beyond what would be easier weakens your spiritual wall of protection. Have you ever noticed yourself singing the words to a hymn or speaking in prayer a request that God would use your life to the fullest and then, in the next moment, hear yourself grumbling that you are inconvenienced, asked to do more than usual, or take on a new responsibility? The call of Jesus includes settling in with a positive outlook on your journey of faith and, like when exercising new muscles at the gym, accepting the temporary discomfort as encouraging spiritual progress. Getting others to sympathize and validate your complaints will not help you grow strong. In fact, it's impossible to complain your way into spiritual fruitfulness. Would others say that your "solution" to a challenge is to complain as often as you can about it? If yes, how effective has that solution been for you?

Another related Upsurge Breakthrough Prayer practice distraction is perceiving yourself always as the **victim**. Think about it: every good story has a victor, a victim, and a villain. As long as you are always looking for the villainous reasons and circumstances that you can claim as reasons that prevent you from spiritual upsurge, they certainly will. However, recasting yourself through this particular breakthrough prayer practice can help you realize that in Christ's power you are instead the victor, anticipating with confidence what God is going to do next or how God will show up in every storyline that unfolds.

Upsurge Prayer distractions can also be ushered in by **times of trouble or stormy seasons**, presenting genuinely difficult life obstacles to navigate. Perhaps you've noticed that some praying believers come out the other side of an unexpected dark valley of unexpected hardship or challenge even stronger and more burnished in faith, having used it as an Upsurge stepping-stone like David to reach "the rock higher than I." Others encounter the furnace of affliction and, taking their eyes off the goal, impoverish the resources of the Holy Spirit by assuming God's abandonment, treating prayer as though it has no efficacy at all, and attempting to crawl through it on their own.

Be assured that when Jesus said, "*In the world you have tribulation, but take courage; I have overcome the world*" (John 16:33 NASB), he was referring to times of trouble entirely capable of distracting your prayer focus. The Greek word Jesus used that's translated as "tribulation" in this verse literally means "pressure" or "pressing together." That's how trouble feels, right? Jesus's strong assertion about overcoming the world utilizes a Greek verb that also intimated conquering and prevailing. Embrace the resurrection hope of Christ in you and ramp up your Upsurge Breakthrough Prayer practice when the stress of a challenge threatens to do the opposite. It's always the path up and out.

You—Together with Ministry Traveling Companions

I hope that Alicia's story validated that, as a leader for Christ, it's crucial to have spiritual "traveling companions" who will listen to you, pray with you, and journey with you in discipleship, and you likewise with them. Spiritual traveling companions—whether through a Bible study, class, committee, choir, or church council—can be those who will join you in courageous breakthrough prayer practices and who also believe, as you do, that prayer makes a difference.

I also wonder if you're thinking that the basic theme you noticed in Alicia's story could be analogous to the paralysis of a team on which you currently serve. In following Jesus together, you may have stepped forward to lead toward a new goal, believing that to be God's preferred direction. You could see the destination in your mind's eye, the view of the eventual accomplishment's purpose. But once you stepped out, it was much more difficult than foreseen. You have found you were ill-equipped or inexperienced to handle the pushback, resistance, or generalized inertia of the congregation or your committee members. There's no sense of God's comforting peace and calm—only challenges and even pain. Your heart may feel as "faint" as David's did as he clung, frustrated, to the highest rock he could manage on his own.

If God is indeed leading, you are underway on an exciting expedition of risky faith and surrender, featuring comfort-zone exceptions and rigors intended for the sole prospect of transforming you and your team into the likeness of Christ. You and your traveling companions are there for a purpose: to encourage each other with humbling,

Spirit-inspired insistence to discard or exchange the disabling baggage of pride, destructive leadership habits, territorialism, defensiveness, or anything else you've been collectively schlepping along in your group dynamics that threaten to discourage or deter you. It's time for the Upsurge Breakthrough Prayer practice, over and over, to become the heartbeat of your leadership journey together.

Upsurge Prayer Handholds (Prayer-holds)

Like Alicia, leaders who practice the Upsurge Breakthrough Prayer, asking God for miraculous resourcing beyond themselves for the accomplishment of reaching the next summit, may also expose the personal specifics of disabling "baggage" hindering their upward climb. Alicia eventually named hers as pride and judgmentalism. How would you name your own baggage or that of your team or council?

If an additional specific Upsurge Breakthrough Prayer word could help you surrender your grip on one or more of your unique impedimenta and gain a new prayer handhold—or prayer-hold—to get moving, here are a few examples to consider. What others come to your mind to add to this list?

Choose.

Maybe your challenge is that you want to say yes to the rock that is higher than you but feel paralyzed to get moving. This Upsurge Prayer-hold comes from Moses's instructions to the children of Israel in Deuteronomy 30:19: *"Now choose life—so that you and your descendants will live"* (CEB). He challenged them to remember that their choice would be the example the next generations would follow.

The specific Hebrew word Moses used, translated in English as "choose," carried with it the emphasis that what is selected should be looked at carefully, tested and found to be the best, most thought-out choice. The Holy Spirit may provide you through this prayer word to gain a push to irresistibly see your next forward step as more excellent than the indecision that hampers you. Spiritual energy is unleashed through the power of choosing to act in faith.

Finish.

Do you engage your faith and will for a new upward climb and then become distracted or falter as your eyes glimpse potential perilous dangers and hazards? You may be prone to stalling out or even turning back, despite your inspired best intentions.

The Upsurge Prayer-hold of **Finish** is based on the original Greek of Philippians 1:6, where Paul writes *"the one who started a good work in you will stay with you to complete [finish] the job by the day of Christ Jesus"* (CEB). What spiritual resources to stay focused on the climb could God unleash in and through you by this single-word breakthrough prayer reminder?

Rock.

This Upsurge Prayer-hold, taken from Psalm 61:2 itself, is also utilized elsewhere in the Old Testament to mean *"strength."* Not only is this prayer-hold useful as a single word breakthrough prayer request for God to provide you the strength you need, it can also give you a mental visual of the solidness of the rock of God who provides your strength.

Discussion or Journal Questions for Application

Upsurge Prayer is a one-sentence (or one-word) breakthrough prayer practice that you can use in moments or seasons when you (and/ or your team) find yourself embarking into—or in the midst of—a new segment of your spiritual path that requires you to learn and grow to rely on God's presence and resources, as well as on yourself, in enlarged ways. These will reshape your faith and trust as you give up what holds you back (old habits, perspectives, and aversions), lean into what your path can teach you spiritually, and let go of the assumptions and expectations of how you will get where God is calling you to go. Upsurge Breakthrough Prayer is costly. It invites openness for God to take you, via miraculous resources, farther on and higher up. Expect the Holy Spirit to utilize unfamiliar new demands, limited or unique resources, irritating or distracting traveling companions, and surprising new growing edges just beyond your comfort zone as venues for miraculous fertilizer that can enable new Fruit of the Spirit to blossom in you.

Together with your group or team (or individually in your journal), imagine that you hold in your hand a rock, stone, or pebble that represents a physical, relational, spiritual, or mental "climb" or seeming impasse that you have potentially faced, or that you face now as a leader, a ministry team, or personally. If you wish, provide yourself and each member of your team or group with a small rock or stone to hold.

1. What has been an occasion (by choice or by circumstances) that you attempted any type of new challenge that was beyond your prior experience or out of your comfort zone? What equipment, supplies, or skills did you wish you would have had, but did not?

2. Did you have any "traveling companions" along on the challenge—and if so, whom? Were your traveling companion(s) helpful; willing; well-partnered to your speed or pace; slowing you down; sprinting ahead; or some other description?

3. Did you find yourself bumping up against any excuses or complaints within yourself that may have slowed you down or stopped you? What were they?

4. What did the new challenge "cost" you—both expected and unexpected? How far did you get and why?

5. How would you describe any spiritual learning or reward, silver lining, or "mountaintop view" that came from attempting the challenge that you named? What did you learn that may have helped you since?

6. What role did your faith and prayer play, if any? Did the challenge discourage your prayer life or deepen it?

7. As you have reflected on the Upsurge Breakthrough Prayer practice, *"Lead me to the rock that is higher than I,"* has the Holy Spirit brought any additional single sentence/phrase prayer-hold variations to mind, in addition to those provided in this chapter? Share them with your group or write them in your journal.

Concluding Prayer Time

As a group (or in your own reflection time after journaling), offer each person a turn that includes the following:

- Give a one-word (or a few-words) name to the "rock" you aspire to now but that will require God's supernatural equipping/shaping and miraculous resourcing to reach. It could be for you as a leader or for the ministry team on which you serve.

- Then name, in a few words, what you have become aware you will need to lay down or let go (excess "baggage") to become more agile and spiritually adept to reach the Master's helpful hand.

- Finally, finish with the one-sentence Upsurge Breakthrough Prayer practice of the heart you intend to practice in the days to come, or your one-word prayer-hold.

15

QUICK-REMINDER SUMMARY #1

The first bead on my own breakthrough prayer practices strand I described in the introductory "Begin Here" chapter is from **Psalm 61:2: Lead Me to the Rock That Is Higher Than I**. This is the one-sentence breakthrough prayer that I pray when I find myself facing a task, scenario, or difficulty that has filled me with uncertainty and I lack what I feel I need to scale it. Although beating a hasty retreat, stepping aside, or just giving up might be the easier options, I use this Upsurge Prayer practice as a request for God to break through with spiritual resources to boost me further than I thought I could, see what I have not seen before, try what I haven't been willing or aware of previously, and free my grip on old stubborn habits and "givens" in order to grow and mature into new ones.

When you reflect on utilizing this verse as an Upsurge Breakthrough Prayer practice, stay focused on what it is you are actually asking of God when you pray this verse. Your request is for God to "grow you up," to mature and lift you to a place in your spiritual transformation beyond where you are now. This is not a prayer asking God to remove the resistant persons or frustrating picayune potholes littering your attempts to become more spiritual. Nor is it a prayer requesting God allow you to stay where you're comfortable or grant you an easier go instead. This is the breakthrough prayer practice for individuals and teams that long to live the spiritual adventure and are willing to pay the cost—which is in faith surrendering all that you've been thus far, moving beyond your level of comfort and self-confidence in trust, stretching farther and expending more effort and energy that you dreamed, in order to indeed reach the rock that is higher—with a God-sized view beyond what you could ask, think, or imagine.

"BE NOT AFRAID" BREAKTHROUGH PRAYER

Be not afraid ... for I am with you;
Do not anxiously look about you, for I am your God.
I will strengthen you, surely I will help you,
Surely I will uphold you with My righteous right hand.

—Isaiah 41:10 (NASB)

WATCH #2 Video Breakthrough Prayer Practice Story: John and Michelle

Find introductory videos featuring true stories that illustrate the
breakthrough prayer practice for each chapter of *Ultimate Reliance* at:
www.cokesbury.com/ultimate-reliance-study

I once heard a Bible professor assert that the most prolific message in scripture, emphasized more often than anything else, is the spiritual directive to *Be Not Afraid*. Later, as these three words became a break-through prayer practice represented by the second bead on my own devotional prayer strand, I have noticed the frequency I find myself praying it. Some days, it may be the most recurrent breakthrough prayer practice to which I turn.

This particular admonishment by Isaiah for the people of Israel not to fear or be afraid (Isaiah 41:10) utilizes the Hebrew verb *Yare'*, varying forms of which appear a whopping 382 times throughout the Old Testament in its original language. The usage of *Yare'* could describe either of two different categories of fear. One was the emotion of dread, terror, or concern for potential harm. The other was for portraying esteem, respect, and worship of God.

17

Bundled together in Isaiah's entreaty for God's followers to "be not afraid," could it be we find a startling inference that within the very same fear or terror-filled moment is also contained the awe-inspiring presence and enabling power of the miraculous God Almighty?

Be Not Afraid. . . .

This second breakthrough prayer practice, then, may encapsulate one of the mysterious blessings of a wholly reliant walk of faith: that as real as fear and anxiety may be on any given occasion in your life as a leader, through this prayer practice you can simultaneously acknowledge, surrender to, and open the floodgates of the undeniable presence of the One who will strengthen, help, and uphold you.

Be Not Afraid: Ministry Leadership

The miracle of this specific "both/and" prayer bundle came together for me when I was a young pastor newly out of seminary. I didn't come face to face with physical danger that elicited fear. It showed up in a different format. Agonizingly, I found myself battling increasing apprehension whenever it was my turn in the pulpit. It manifested by stumbling over words, keeping my eyes glued to the sermon manuscript, and unsuccessfully wrestling with an internal sense of failure and a "what are people thinking about me?" dread. It all left me ready to shed private tears when Sunday morning worship was finally over. The anxiety eventually took root as full-blown fear. I remember confessing to those around me that it seemed my pastoral call might eventually no longer include preaching and speaking before others. The fright and terror was exhausting and defeating me.

One of the faith-filled members of my congregation at the time happened to be a sports psychologist. Following what must have been Spirit-inspired intuition, he approached me one Sunday after having observed me up front during the service.

"You're afraid, aren't you?" he asked directly. Emotion and embarrassment welled up inside. Then humiliation Then the familiar fear. I couldn't reply.

I'll always remember his game-changing next words. "You have found you have an enormous capacity for fear, haven't you? But please hear this. You also have an equally enormous capacity for God confidence. What you do as a pastor is far and away more spiritually significant than the athletes I work with as they battle their competition fears and learn to manage them productively. I hope you take heart when I tell you that it's possible for you to learn to replace your 'panic prompts' with new 'courage and confidence' prompts. I'll bet then that the Holy Spirit will take care of the rest. If you'd like some help finding your way past your fears, here's my business card and we'll give it a try."

Over the next few weeks, I developed trepidation about actually facing the fear. But I set up a meeting with my parishioner. What would it finally take for me to embrace and live the scriptural instructions to *Be Not Afraid*? I had to find out.

The Breakthrough Relationship between Fear and Faith

I hope by now as you read this, you are thinking about your own occasions that are capable of triggering fear in you. It may not be speaking or preaching in front of a gathering of people, as it was for me. Most of us, when describing a moment when we've been afraid, can describe physical symptoms our particular fear generates: goosebumps; butterflies in the gut; a flash of adrenaline to fight, run, or spout off; or a desire to melt down, shout, cry, or retreat. Hands tremble or turn cold, teeth might chatter. Voices quiver. Memory falters. There is a struggle for focus. Fatigue. Sense of disconsolation. Discouragement. Nausea.

What I learned from the sports psychologist made a profound new contribution to my breakthrough prayer practices. I discovered that while I always prayed prior to stepping up to the pulpit, that's where my actual praying ended. The sight of the expectant faces of my congregation ready to hear a meaningful sermon directly provoked negative self-talk inside me ("Oh my! They are going to think I am doing a terrible job. I am not gifted for this. My sermon won't make sense. This is going to be awful!"). Fear emotions would then manifest in the outplay of bumbling words, an inability to focus, and trembling hands. I finally comprehended that this had become a self-fulfilling and debilitating cycle that a breakthrough prayer practice, the missing ingredient of God's redemptive Spirit, needed ongoing opportunities to disrupt.

I still remember the landmark Sunday morning when I took the familiar few steps into the pulpit to preach. But instead of looking out at the congregation or down at my sermon notes, I first looked at a card I'd placed just beside them. It read *Be Not Afraid*.

And in the pause before starting to speak, I closed my eyes and silently prayed that breakthrough prayer to myself multiple times. Miraculously, I sensed the peace of God's Spirit as it began to trickle through me. When I finally looked at those seated in the pews and began the message, the tenacious old negative self-talk thoughts attempted to rise. But I kept glancing at the breakthrough prayer card repeatedly as a touchpoint. What a miracle! When I finished preaching that morning, it was with the start of a hope that through the diligent discipline of this new prayer practice disrupting the fear sequence, I might one day be set free indeed.

What I know now from experience is that by inviting God consistently into our fears via a habitual breakthrough prayer practice, gradually a gush of divine strength finds its way up, over, and around whatever threatens to deter it. In my case, it was entrenched fear activated by accompanying negative self-talk. For you, it might be deploying the breakthrough prayer practice of *Be Not Afraid* in a sudden unexpected moment of danger or threat. We could say that through the power of this particular breakthrough prayer practice, the rivers of Living Water can flow between the banks of your fear.

The Definition of "Spiritual Disciplines"

Facing this particular fear has been an ongoing journey of personal regeneration over time. These days, I still have occasions of feeling fear when I'm preparing to speak or to lead trainings. And it comes as no surprise that if I have neglected the Be Not Afraid Breakthrough Prayer practice beforehand and during, the negative, anxiety-filled self-talk of failure and defeat speaks up as though it had never taken a break. I now simply let that internal voice be a prompt to recommence the consistent discipline of replacing it with the Be Not Afraid Prayer practice, through which God continues liberating and transforming me.

According to Christian history, "spiritual disciplines" are practices or spiritual habits modeled in the life of Christ that, if practiced consistently, God will use to shape us into ever more of Christ's likeness. One of the classic spiritual disciples is prayer. Luke records that Jesus, facing distractions by the voice of Satan to compromise or derail his earthly calling, used scripture verses as breakthrough prayer-like invitations for God's presence and truth (Matthew 4:1-8). As a result, angels showed up to be present and minister to his needs! In the same way, replacing the distracting voice of your unique fears with a breakthrough prayer like Isaiah's words "Be Not Afraid" is an invitation for God's prevailing presence. It's not just different self-talk. It's a request for the Holy Spirit to take charge. You move from talking to yourself to inviting supernatural possibilities.

Oswald Chambers, Scottish Bible teacher and author of the daily devotional *My Utmost for His Highest*, was convinced that though our first conversion is surrendering to Christ, the process of "continuous conversion" through the consistent practice of new spiritual habits or disciplines is an ongoing necessity. But it's not easy.

> The relation of the natural to the spiritual is one of continuous conversion, and it is the one thing we object to. In every setting in which we are put, the Spirit of God remains unchanged and His salvation unaltered but we have to "put on the new man" [Ephesians 4:20-24]. . . . The hindrance in our spiritual life is that we will not be continually converted, there are "wadges" of obstinacy where our pride spits at the throne of God and says—"I won't."
> (*My Utmost for His Highest*, classic version, December 28 entry)

You—Together with Ministry Traveling Companions

The people of Israel to whom Isaiah initially spoke the words of Isaiah 41:10 were both literal and spiritual traveling companions, seeking to find their way together as they grappled with danger, shortage of resources, transitions, change, enemies who threatened to defeat them, and disagreements amongst themselves. Isaiah's words were a bold reassurance that God would be with them in the fear-filled times to come with provision for what they would need. Is it any wonder that internet sources report, even today, this verse is one of the most often-shared year over year?

You and your ministry colleagues face modern versions of the same challenges on your leadership journey. Recognizing, owning, and praying through feelings of fear is core to effective collaboration. Otherwise, the fear-prompted self-talk that gets promulgated among you—and even influences your meeting agenda—almost guarantees your church will remain plateaued, or possibly slide into decline. Whatever your investment for Christ's work—whether you're on staff at your church, part of a ministry group, or a teacher in a Christian Education program—not allowing the adverse effects of fear to short-change you is a high-priority breakthrough prayer challenge.

The diversity of Hebrew Old Testament (and Greek New Testament) words that scholars have translated as "fear" or "afraid" is a reminder of how many guises fear can assume. Fear can hide itself in even the most rationalized or respectable attitudes and assumptions.

For example, maybe your team has succumbed to a fear-filled **"martyr" mentality**, believing that there's nothing you can do right because everyone always blames you, so it is best to not make waves. Just keep your heads down, care for the financials and the building, and wait until it's your turn to rotate out of leadership. No one appreciates your work anyway.

Or maybe you struggle with **procrastination**—self-talk triggered by fear that provides what may seem like perfectly reasonable, but foundationally ruinous, excuses not to care for your responsibilities in a timely manner. This version of fear might emanate when you look at your lengthy to-do list, for example. Your real fear is usually not a task itself. Listen closely to what the inhibiting voice inside is rationalizing in order to find out.

A prospective change or new project that precipitates endless hours of discussion prolonged by a supercharged undercurrent of **fear of the unknown future** could derail your team. Your group's self-talk in the discussion might repeatedly emphasize every conceivable drawback, pitfall, and harmful consequence that might happen. Remember the rich young ruler who approached Jesus, as recounted in Mark 10:17-22? His fear arose quickly when he was asked to make changes and follow Jesus more fully. What do you imagine his inner voice must have been saying about the dangers of giving away his predictable, comfortable material resources in order to shift to new priorities and unfamiliar action?

As Jesus continued down the road, a man ran up, knelt before him, and asked, "Good Teacher, what must I do to obtain eternal life?"

Jesus replied, "Why do you call me good? No one is good except the one God. You know the commandments: Don't commit murder. Don't commit adultery. Don't steal. Don't give false testimony. Don't cheat. Honor your father and mother."

"Teacher," he responded, "I've kept all of these things since I was a boy."

Jesus looked at him carefully and loved him. He said, "You are lacking one thing. Go, sell what you own, and give the money to the poor. Then you will have treasure in heaven. And come, follow me." But the man was dismayed at this statement and went away saddened, because he had many possessions. (CEB)

Or for your team it might be noxious inner self-talk that started **in the past** when something in church life didn't turn out as hoped. Thus, today's decisions and opportunities are tainted with refrains of what didn't happen back then, resulting in fear-filled amnesia around what God has indeed accomplished in and through you collectively over time. Another offshoot of this fear might be listening to the shared self-talk of shortage and scarcity, rather than investing in confident prayers for God's supernatural and abundant provision.

Prejudice is yet another self-talk-fueled outplay of fear. Narratives by the critical inner voice may then speak false judgments and suspicion about those who are different than we are, and it becomes a contagiously fear-filled groupthink.

Have any of these fear versions contaminated your leadership or your ministry team's progress, dissuaded your courage, or persuaded you to retreat instead of advance?

Whatever it might be that triggers your fear as a leader, as a team, or in your personal life, decide you will replace the negative self-talk or team-talk with a breakthrough prayer practice that becomes revolutionary.

Be Not Afraid Prayer Handholds (Prayer-holds)

As you're now aware, fear can appear wearing a variety of disguises. Be ready to recognize and name defeating "inner voices" if any of these expressions of fear are evident in your attitude and perspective or that of your team. Begin the spiritual discipline of habitually replacing each of them with a prayer word handhold, or "prayer-hold," that God can use to bring spiritual conversion. In addition to *Be Not Afraid*, here are other ideas.

Strength.

The voice of your fear may have been self-talking overtime to convince you that you've been overlooked by others, by circumstances, or by your own perceived lack of support or appreciation. These are excuses for staying an immobilized prisoner to your fears. A single prayer-word practice useful to replace your inner "victim" commentary could be "*Strength.*" Remember Philippians 4:13: "*I can do all things through [Christ] who strengthens me*" (NASB).

Accomplish.

When you fearfully find yourself putting off what should be done now, call procrastination by its rightful name. Use this prayer-hold to replace the excuses you have made to yourself, and embrace Jesus's own prayer in John 17:4: "*I have glorified you on earth by finishing the work you gave me to do*" (CEB).

Streams.

This prayer word is a rich reminder when your overwhelming fear generates an inner negative voice convincing you that God's Spirit is nowhere to be found. It comes from Jesus's words to his disciples in John 7:38: "*He who believes in Me, as the Scripture said, 'From his innermost being will flow rivers [streams] of living water'*" (NASB).

Abundance.

Feelings of fear often lead to "scarcity" self-talk, and your eyes then perceive nothing but shortage and limitations. Yet our faith assures us that in the spiritual realm we have a Great Provider. This prayer word is rooted in Ephesians 3:20, where Paul wrote about the One "*who is able to do far more abundantly beyond all that we ask or think, according to the power that works within us*" (NASB).

Discussion or Journal Questions for Application

Be Not Afraid is a one-sentence breakthrough prayer practice that you can use in moments or seasons when you (and/or your team) are slowed or held back by fears that have convinced you God's activity isn't present or imminent. Fear may spring up when you need to do something in which you are not confident. Maybe it appears when you need to visit someone critically ill in the hospital, or teach a class for the first time or on an unfamiliar subject. It could spring up when you need to handle what you know will be a conversation with someone who can get loud and angry. Fear might be fueled by the past: an action for which you need to ask forgiveness, or a memory of when you were adversely wronged. And, as has already been described, fear also affects groups and teams. It's time to live the discovery—as I did—that your worst fear, as Isaiah pointed out, actually comes bundled together with the presence and power of God.

Place an empty chair at your table or in the center of the room. Invite yourself, or each person in your group, to imagine that a self-identified fear motivator is seated in the empty chair.

1. What is the name of a circumstance, reality, task, responsibility, or potential, big or small, that you imagine seated in that chair? Is it new or has it been around for a long time?

What fears is it capable of prompting in you? What is the self-talk that is then generated?

(If you cannot identify anything to imagine in the chair, simply listen closely as others share. Part of your own fear-induced self-talk might be that you must deny the existence of any of your own. It's possible now that God may help you gradually recognize a fear in yourself that has been hidden.)

2. Think about your life's "traveling companions," at church or personally, who regularly surround you. Is there anyone who is or has (intentionally or inadvertently) validated or multiplied your fears and contributed negatively to the self-talk in your mind?

Conversely, has anyone suggested powerful replacement scripture or prayer truths for you to consider as a break-through prayer practice to disrupt a fear sequence you are experiencing? If so, what?

3. Look, in your mind's eye, at what you have seated in the chair. What, if anything, might your resultant fears and self-talk have cost you in terms of progress on your spiritual path of faith?

4. Sometimes our fears actually become like a well-known housemate. We accept the compromised consequences they deliver and acclimate to them. On a scale of 1 (low) to 10 (high), what is the honest level of your motivation and resolve to establish a new breakthrough prayer practice discipline when any particular fear feelings arise, and why? What would it take for you to decide to begin?

5. This chapter provides *Be Not Afraid*, as well as several other prayer-hold suggestions, to replace the self-talk that fears prompt. Are any of these prayer-holds a fit for you? Can you think of any others that fit here?

6. Describe the outcome that might unfold if, through this breakthrough prayer practice, you did become "fearless" (not necessarily free of fear, but with a new prayer practice that opens God's floodgates with a flow of Living Water to replace the negative inner voice causing feelings of fear). What might change if you were fully confident God was active and right there with you?

7. Look again at the empty chair, and imagine what is seated there. But this time, look at it from your congregation or your team's perspective of your current shared work and challenges. How would you describe what you see?

8. Discuss or journal about what single-sentence version of breakthrough prayer you could collectively embrace to allow God to change limitations into holy momentum.

Concluding Prayer Time

As a group, offer each person a turn that includes the following:

- Pray aloud the Be Not Afraid Breakthrough Prayer or a one-word prayer-hold that you intend to practice as a spiritual discipline in the days to come.

- If you are utilizing this as your team or group's resource, do a second go-around so that each person may also pray a specific Be Not Afraid Prayer or word for your group or congregation's needs. Alternately, invite your team leader to do this on everyone's behalf.

QUICK-REMINDER SUMMARY #2

The second bead on my own breakthrough prayer practices strand I described in the introductory "Begin Here" chapter is from **Isaiah 41:10: Be Not Afraid.** This is the one-sentence breakthrough prayer that I pray when I find myself feeling fear that's followed by apprehensive or self-critical mental chatter that ramps up my anxiety, bankrupting the God-confidence to act. This is a powerful prayer spiritual discipline to embrace whenever you notice yourself experiencing symptoms of fear. Practice intentionally replacing the inner voice that's prompting them with a Be Not Afraid Breakthrough Prayer practice instead.

The actual feelings of fear may never fully subside. But you'll discover that in the midst of fear, as in the Hebrew word *Yare'*, is equally the place where the awe and wonder of God can also break forth and take shape.

"LET THERE BE LIGHT" BREAKTHROUGH PRAYER

Then God said, "Let there be light"; and there was light. God saw that the light was good; and God separated the light from the darkness.

—*Genesis 1:3-4 (NASB)*

WATCH #3 Video Breakthrough Prayer Practice Story: Dan

Find introductory videos featuring true stories that illustrate the breakthrough prayer practice for each chapter of *Ultimate Reliance* at: www.cokesbury.com/ultimate-reliance-study

---

My husband, an airline pilot, often describes the dramatic visual change through the cockpit window as his aircraft lifts off, gains altitude, and then moves up, through, and beyond a dark and threatening cloud cover to the brilliant sunshine and clear sky above. It's as though a gloomy and foggy atmospheric environment evident on takeoff is elevated in a matter of minutes to an entirely different perspective. The clouds that appeared troubling and adversarial when observed from the ground are now sparkling beauty from the upward side, reflecting the bright light of the sun. The previously expressed angst of the planeload of passengers buckled in back behind him ("Will the plane be able to take off in this weather? Through those clouds? Is it safe?") shifts to calm and relief. What a real-life illustration this is for our next breakthrough prayer practice: *Let There Be Light.*

The opening verses of the Bible's first book, Genesis, have a poetic beauty in the description of God's creative activity forming the world as we know it. The first shaping that God spoke into existence was the creation of light and the separation from darkness. The themes of light and darkness reverberate from here as a recurring theme across both the Old and New Testament. In spiritual alignment, light and darkness thus emerge as overarching guideposts for us as leaders on the journey of breakthrough prayer.

The Hebrew word used in the third and fourth verses of the first chapter of Genesis, referring to the *light* God created, is also translated elsewhere in scripture as "illumination," "enlightenment," and "wisdom." The Hebrew word rendered here in Genesis as *darkness* appears around eighty times in the Old Testament, in some contexts indicating obscurity, falsehood, or ignorance. Its figurative meaning in places infers blindness, hiddenness, or judgment.

Clearly, in God's intentional separation of light from darkness, we are given nomenclature for that which we seek: who among us doesn't long for God's Spirit to bring us the light of supernatural clarity, rather than the darkness of confusion and uncertainty?

But our human experience of following Christ on earth simply doesn't offer the uninhibited brilliance of the clear directional view in every moment. We occasionally find ourselves like the airline passengers, peering through inclement and potentially dangerous atmospheric conditions in day-to-day living and leading. We struggle and speculate on how to navigate through. We delay our departure or may even cancel making decisions. If scripture is clear, however, that "God is light, and there is no darkness in him at all" (1 John 1:5 CEB), how do we wrap our prayers and our faith around situations and seasons in which God's light doesn't seem evident?

Spiritual Weather Forecast: Darkness, Clouds, and Shadows

In both ministry leadership and in personal prayer life, the simple Let There Be Light Breakthrough Prayer practice invites the Almighty's divine hand to separate the darkness from the light. It's a request for God to bring clearness, direction, and revelation to what is before us, beyond what we can see ourselves with our own human understanding and assumptions. When you or I have said yes to God's call to lead, serve, befriend, teach, or love, it's human to expect that God's response is to bless us with the sunny, sparkling, cloudless joy of fulfilling the call.

So if God has beckoned forward, is darkness a sudden sign of God's disfavor? Far from it! In Psalm 119:147, the author wrote that even in the dark, prior to his customary prayer watch that came at sunrise, *"I rise before dawn and cry for help; I wait for Your words"* (NASB). In fact, the next verse adds that *"My eyes anticipate the night watches, that I may meditate on Your word."* We have the capacity to learn to value the darkness as a time to allow God's Spirit to dwell deep in us through scripture as we prepare with expectation for light's arrival. In fact, darkness and other spiritual weather conditions become invaluable utensils in God's hand to continue the sculpting of spiritual growth and maturity.

First, let's affirm that though this breakthrough prayer practice may be for light, God's word clearly reflects that **both light and darkness** have value as we pray and journey spiritually.

In *Flood Gates: Holy Momentum for a Fearless Church*, I wrote about Mother Teresa's prayer life. One of the great "prayer warriors" of our generation, she kept countless prayer journals that chronicled a passionate daily prayer life throughout her entire vocational ministry years. The fruitfulness God brought through her to impact so many lives with God's tangible love became legendary.

Most would assume that Mother Teresa enjoyed a brilliantly lit partnership with God through her prayer dedication. But ten years after her death in 1997, we learned differently when a book of her personal letters, taken from her prolific prayer journals, was published. *Mother Teresa: Come Be My Light* (2007, Doubleday) revealed that her prayer life for many years had been "dark"—without any sense of the light of God's presence at all. Yet Mother Teresa always continued to pray, even in what she named as years of unemotional blank darkness. And in hindsight it's evident that God continued to work powerfully, consistently, and faithfully in and through her prayers whether she felt God alongside or not.

It's crucial for those who pray to keep this awareness: there will be times of prayer that feel full of God's light and presence—**lights-on prayer**—as well as times when no presence of God can be sensed—**lights-off prayer**. God, however, is equally attentive and responsive during both. Continue to pray with confidence and faith, whether the "light" of God's presence feels on or off.

33

Cherish this truth in your own breakthrough prayer life. On occasions you feel or sense only darkness, the God who created the light is still fully present. Embrace this from the prayer of **Psalm 139:11-12**.

> *If I say, "Surely the darkness will overwhelm me,*
> *And the light around me will be night,"*
> *Even the darkness is not dark to You,*
> *And the night is as bright as the day.*
> *Darkness and light are alike to You.* (NASB)

Second, let's note that the themes of darkness and light that wind through scripture also involve **shadows**. Have you ever found that your prayers seem to point the way to next steps that aren't in full view? If you find yourself or your ministry team on a shadowy path, frustrated that the way forward isn't more clearly apparent, remember that shadows are cast because of a light source nearby. Though there may be shadows, your assurance is that the full light of God shines just adjacent to whatever casts the shadow that concerns you. "*Yea, though I walk in the valley of the shadow of death, I fear no evil; for you are with me...*" (Ps 23:4 NASB).

Another value of shadows is that they help draw our attention to what is actually in the **light.** Like a videographer who carefully adjusts bulbs, screens, and sheers so that what is filmed will be featured by defining light—and what is less important will fade into the shadows— so the Holy Spirit may take advantage of shadowy, obscured parts of our daily walk of faith, using what isn't clear to draw our attention to what is God's illumined priority or insight for us. The Let There Be Light Breakthrough Prayer practice may not be answered with a spiritual sensation that the entire bank of "house lights" have been turned on in your life's stadium. Cultivate gratitude for the shadows. Work on looking for where God has brought light, rather than becoming preoccupied or frustrated with what the shadows currently conceal. And act on the light, however limited, that you do see. The light will then spread farther before you.

If the "shadows" that fringe your prayers for God's light to break through seem tenacious, perhaps you might consider whether they are actually present as protection. David, while traversing the wilderness in escape from enemies, penned a prayer giving thanks for the "shadow"

34

of God's wings (Psalm 63:7 NASB), using a Hebrew word that was also used to describe "safe shelter." In fact, David's prayer was that he would "sing for joy" in the shadow. The author of Psalm 91 also used the same Hebrew word to affirm the choice to "abide in the shadow of the Almighty." Might the shadow season in which you find yourself actually be a protective gift for now?

Third, the light and darkness motifs throughout God's word also include **clouds**. Occasionally, when praying *Let There Be Light*, you may feel as though you're attempting to drive down the highway of your life in the fog, wrestling with the stress and frustration of dense clouds occluding your view. You're not sure what, if anything, might be hidden in the clouds and fog just ahead, making any movement forward seem risky. It's possible as church leaders, and in your own following of Christ, that opaque clouds of unknown content are blocking your way.

Or are they? Oswald Chambers wrote this about the nature of clouds.

> In the Bible clouds are always connected with God....If there were no clouds, we should have no faith. The clouds are but the dust of our Father's feet. The clouds are a sign that He is there. (*My Utmost for His Highest*, classic version, July 29 entry)

What if the "clouds" that may seem like chaos to you are simply evidence of God's active presence—dust of the Master's feet? Would your attitude toward them change? Luke 9:34-36 offers an account of the disciples Peter, John, and James, who went up the mountain with Christ to pray. While there, *"a cloud formed and began to overshadow them; and they were afraid as they entered the cloud"* (9:34 NASB). But upon having the courage to enter, they discovered only Jesus in the cloud. Could it be that the "clouds" holding you back from stepping forward also contain only Jesus, who is eager to meet you there so you can proceed together?

Let There Be Light: A Two-Sided Breakthrough Prayer

As you begin to practice this third breakthrough prayer practice in your leadership and also as a tool for your own discipleship, be aware that this prayer is not only outward-focused. Yes, you may feel a spiritual tug to pray *Let There Be Light* in moments when you and others need God's supernatural light to shine clearly enough to help you see your circumstances and gain wisdom. But at the same time, this prayer for God's light is also a request for the light to shine inward. The crevasses, clefts, crannies, and locked closets of your heart and spirit that comprise your inner self may be harboring destructive darkness that needs to be revealed and removed so that you are more capable of outwardly discerning God's light. The light you seek that shows the way forward may already be shining, but you could be spiritually "blinded" by what remains inside you shrouded in darkness.

Jesus, well aware that inner darkness can prevent our visibility of God's light at work around us, spoke more than once about the necessity of God's transforming light to also shine into our inner spiritual life. *"What I tell you in the darkness, speak in the light,"* he proclaimed (Matthew 10:27 NASB), referencing the conversions of thought and attitudes that come via our own spiritual housecleaning. A psalmist wrote the same directive: *"Light arises [breaks through] in the darkness for the upright"* (Psalm 112:4 NASB).

The light of God's direction you can potentially see outward will only become more apparent as you grow in your resolve to ask for God's light to invade and transform your interior comfort zone of negative attitudes, judgmentalism, prejudice, complacency, or unforgiveness. Otherwise, you'll see God's light around you through distorted prescription lenses. Praying *Let There Be Light* requires spiritual courage. As much as you and I might like the clouds or shadows to disappear and allow the brilliance of a spiritual sunbeam to guide us each day, relinquishing personal stubbornness and resistance so that God can unleash the new life of Christ living within is the companion requirement. May God find us willing servants to yield as the Light of the World alive in us penetrates deeply, and we weather the life-giving growing pains of ongoing transformational conversions of every kind of light.

Let There Be Light: Ministry Leadership

Pastor Jaxon was excited about his new pastoral appointment. Faith Church sat amidst a transitional neighborhood with newcomers moving in from a variety of multiethnic backgrounds. The tall steeple of the historic building, to Jaxon, appeared to tower over the surrounding residential blocks as a visible symbol of a place where God's love and message could emanate. Even better, he had heard that a core of committed members had launched a small food panty within the previous year. That encouraged him to hope that the congregation had awareness of the needs of its changing community.

Pastor Jaxon did discover the church had an inkling that its neighborhood had changed—but they used it as a reason to grieve. During his first months as the congregation's pastor, he heard story after story from lifelong members that there had been a decade of years, now some time ago, when all the Sunday school downstairs classrooms had been filled with children and the adults had needed to cram themselves into the extra spaces around the building for their own classes. Back then the congregation had all lived in the neighborhood. Now those children were grown and mostly gone. Their parents had retreated to newer suburbs or retirement complexes. The blue parlor window drapery was worn and tattered in places, but in the eyes of the longtime leaders it was still just as beautiful and new as when money had been raised to purchase and install it proudly, nearly twenty-five years prior. It was as though Faith Church members still had faith, but it was attached to the yesteryear memories visible in their rearview mirror.

One of Jaxon's early efforts was to call a meeting of the team members who were responsible for the food pantry. He learned from them that it was a small committee of three persons, and that the food pantry was actually a cart with various donated canned goods that was wheeled to the church's side door on Saturday mornings. Persons who had become aware of the offering by word of mouth would gather outside the side door and wait for the thirty-minute timeframe when the cart would be pushed down the hall to the door's entrance. Rain or shine, they would line up outside, often with children alongside, to receive a small bag of food cans. As the cart emptied each week, the last person in line usually received an odds-and-ends combination, "whatever might still be left in the cart," the committee chair told Pastor Jaxon. He heard that the last Sunday of each month there was always a note put in the worship bulletin, reminding the congregation to "clean out your home pantry" of anything extra to bring to restock the food pantry cart. When Jaxon asked why the line of people was left to stand waiting outside rather than inside the church, the three committee members replied that it was more efficient that way. After all, they explained, a bag could be handed to each quickly, so that the work could be done and the volunteers could get back home without needing to overinvest their time. On Saturdays the volunteers had football to watch, yardwork to do in the warmer months, and other personal weekend activities that beckoned.

After Jaxon had pastored Faith Church through the fall, in January he invited all church leaders to a planning retreat for the new year. He brought along updated statistics to share and discuss about their changing neighborhood, including the shift in economics of the community and the church's own declining attendance trends over the last five, ten, and fifteen years. As he expected, the conversation kept drifting back to the members who had moved away, rather than latching on to the new reality of who lived close by now. An additional topic of concern raised by some was the increase in crime in the blocks surrounding the church.

The most practical and urgent agenda item, however, was the state of the side hallway of the church facility. While performing leaky pipe repairs, a plumber had discovered black mold in the aging ceiling plaster. Mitigation would be necessary as soon as possible.

"But what will happen to the food pantry cart on Saturdays? We always park it inside the side door to the church. That's where the people know to line up and wait," Miriam asked. "If the mitigation work makes the side hallway off limits for a few months, I suppose we can just quit the food cart until the hallway is functional again. Not that many people come anyway. Mostly just those three families, right?" she said to the other two food pantry committee members, sitting at her table. "I'm not sure their names. What's the mother's name who brought along a new baby this last week? Is it Jeannie? Jackie? Whatever. You know which one I mean, the one with dark hair. Her kids are always so loud. Well, we can just tell them this week that we are closing down for awhile."

Jaxon spoke up. "Why cancel the food pantry? Let's move it downstairs to one of the empty classrooms. I think we have at least five rooms downstairs that sit vacant. We could actually turn one of the classrooms into a literal food pantry with shelves, so that those who need food could select what they would like rather than just receiving a bag that's been pre-filled."

"Pastor, that's a nice idea—but you have just spent the last hour showing us statistics about our changing neighborhood and the neighbors we need to reach." Miriam's voice sounded defensive. "Seems like we need to focus on that, rather than trying to turn our food cart into an actual food pantry that looks like a little grocery store or something. We would have to work to get additional food donations to fill the shelves, if we built some in one of the downstairs classrooms. And also, that means that the people coming for the food pantry would need to actually come inside the church and down the stairs. They might need to use our restrooms after the janitor has already cleaned them in preparation for Sunday morning and gone home. And their children are usually not well behaved. We have to think about potential damage that might occur. With this new mitigation issue before us, we don't have extra money for other repairs. I just don't think this is where our energy needs to go."

But Henry, one of Miriam's other two food pantry committee members, seemed energized. "Now that I'm retired, I love the idea of building shelves. My wife says I need more to do these days. I'll build some shelves in one of the downstairs classrooms, if some of the rest of you in this room can help us find grocery stores or other outlets that will donate more food to fill them. That way we can keep it going even while the mitigation work is in process in the side hallway. They can enter through the front church door and come right down the steps to the classroom."

Miriam persisted. "Well, this is just not a great idea. But if we absolutely have to try it, we will also need to turn a second classroom into a 'holding area' for them, while they take turns choosing their groceries. That way we can keep the kids from racing up and down the halls. We have that set of old folding chairs we were going to donate to Goodwill still in the fellowship hall storage closet. We can set up some of those in the second classroom so they can sit and wait in line. I'm not sure about them using our front door, that's all. That's our best reception area for potential church visitors, so we can make a good first impression on Sundays. If this church wants to grow, we have got to keep that nice. I'm not feeling clear that this is a good plan for Faith Church. Seems like there are going to be a number of issues with Pastor Jaxon's suggestions, and I'm not sure why we want to go to this extra effort just for a few people. I'm not even sure where they come from or where they live."

Jaxon just smiled. "The downstairs classrooms are empty, so why not make use of a couple of them? Let's give it a try."

Pastor Jaxon closed the planning retreat by leading the entire group on a prayer-walk through the church building, asking God to break through with new possibilities, hopes, and dreams for the congregation—and especially for God to give the congregation the clarifying light to see how to welcome its neighbors in new and pro-active ways. They lingered in the downstairs classrooms the longest, praying silently and spiritually preparing the space with their prayers. As they finished, Henry happened to exit the soon-to-be food pantry classroom near Miriam. He saw unhappiness and skepticism on her face as she shook her head disapprovingly at the pastor.

Several other leaders present that day did volunteer to check the community for donated food items so that the new shelves to be built by Henry could be filled. Henry donated the lumber and begin construction on simple wooden shelves. That week he also carried several of the old folding chairs to the classroom next door that had been designated as the "holding" room for the food-pantry users. He noticed that the padding on them was ripped and flattened, but he told himself that there were so few persons who typically came to the food pantry that no one would be seated on the chairs for long anyway. He remembered a phone call from Miriam just the day before. "Let's remember that the second classroom is only a waiting area for them," she had said. "The church kitchen is up the stairs and all the way across the front hallway, which is way too inconvenient a distance to think about making coffee to carry down there for them or anything like that. I know how you think, Henry. But let's just let them get their food and get going. We don't need to be doing something like trying to make them coffee. It would take extra time, and there are only three of us on the committee."

The mitigation crews had sealed off the side hallway within two weeks, which caused quick action to stock the shelves in the downstairs classroom and get prepared for the following Saturday morning shift of location and new logistics. Henry arrived an hour early, his favorite Saturday morning cup of Starbucks in hand, in order to prayer-walk the new food pantry classroom and the holding room himself. As he stood in the holding room, asking God to fill it with the spirit of Christ's love, he became aware of the warmth of his coffee cup in hand and its comforting aroma. And he thought how welcome a hot cup of coffee might be to their small collection of food pantry recipients who would be arriving soon. Despite Miriam's instructions, he raced up to the church kitchen and brewed enough coffee to fill two large carafes. He had just carried them downstairs and set them on a card table in the holding room, along with some paper cups, when Miriam arrived.

"Henry, why did you do that? I told you we are not going to make that extra effort for these folks. We don't want to prolong the time we are here this morning by adding extra bells and whistles that they will start expecting! Besides, I signed up to join the Sunday morning greeter team before the weekly worship service as we get better prepared to welcome new visitors and make them feel really at home so they will want to return. That means I have to arrive here even earlier tomorrow, which makes me want to streamline the time we spend with this on Saturday mornings. For this church to survive and turn around our decline, we just have to figure out how to truly welcome our neighbors who come to Sunday worship. That's our number-one priority."

Clouds seemed to part inside Henry's mind as a flash of light-filled insight broke through. "Miriam. Miriam! What if these food-pantry folks are the very neighbors we need to welcome? What if these are the new visitors God is bringing to Faith Church? If they are, they need the same kind of loving welcome as you and the greeter team are planning for tomorrow morning before the worship service!"

Miriam resisted. "These are our neighbors? I don't think so. We don't even know where they live or if they have a permanent address or anything. I know they show up every week for the cans of food, but I'm not sure if we should think they are our 'neighbors.' That's not what I meant."

But Henry's paradigm had shifted, and he felt urgent to help Miriam discover the same. "Miriam, is it really up to us to define who our 'neighbors' should be or what they should be like? Or is our responsibility to simply welcome, in the name and love of Jesus, whomever

God brings to us whether on Saturday or Sunday—or any day of the week?"

At that moment, the first food-pantry family came down the hallway, unfamiliar with the new layout and location. Henry rushed to greet them and to guide them into their new "Welcome Room," as he called it, for coffee and conversation. Miriam returned to her duty post in the food-pantry classroom, struck with a deep conviction and awareness of her own prejudice and judgmentalism regarding the food pantry families they had served over the last year. How, she wondered with self-disappointment, could she have somehow assumed that the food pantry couldn't possibly be the venue through which God might bring an increasing stream of neighbors to honor, welcome, and befriend? And what if God's intention was for the food pantry to become the epicenter of an entire Faith Church makeover, providing an entry point into worship attendance, friendships, membership, and service?

Four months later, the holding room featured a beautiful hand-lettered "Welcome" sign above the door. New comfortable furniture, freshly painted walls, and soft music played every Saturday morning. Hot coffee and homemade breakfast goods were plentiful. The food pantry committee numbers had tripled, with rotating teams who not only helped food-pantry guests gather their preferred food items but also had conversation and prayer, if requested, in the Welcome Room together. In a third classroom, Bible stories and learning activities were available for children while their parents gathered their food items and shared fellowship. Pastor Jaxon often stopped by to get acquainted with the church's neighbors as well, and on Sundays he was amazed to see the food-pantry volunteers seated with an increasing number of food-pantry clients they had invited to worship. By the summer, six people in the Faith Church new members' class had come to the congregation through the food pantry. Even more were part of the new members' class the following fall.

And, best of all, Faith Church's towering steeple had become recognizable in its changing community as the church with the food pantry. Henry found he had to arrive extra early on Saturdays if he wanted to beat Miriam to the classrooms to prayer-walk through them. He often found her kneeling in the Welcome Room by the refreshment table, asking fervently from her heart that Christ's love would illumine them all.

Let There Be Light....

You—Together with Ministry Traveling Companions

You and your ministry colleagues leverage consideration of light and darkness throughout nearly every aspect of your church's existence. Did you realize this?

For example, physical decisions have been made about how your worship area or sanctuary will be physically lit—how brightly or what level of shadowy dimness to better accentuate the worship focus. You may have a cross hanging above the altar, and lights may have been carefully placed so that it is highlighted. Other tangible building decisions made by you, or by leaders before you, may have resulted in the style and placement of stained-glass windows that filter the outside light streaming through them for a meditative appeal. Wall colors of hallways and classrooms can impact a sense of light, mystery, energy, calm, warmth, or disconnect. Even the appearance and placement of interior and exterior building signage impacts passersby's impression of joy-filled light, or a more subdued or even drab mystique of your church.

Like the physical atmosphere, the spiritual atmosphere that's intentionally created by your leadership can also bring the congregation an ongoing awareness that the hope-filled light of Christ is always present to resource and guide, even when "shadows" or "clouds" (without or within us) result in momentary or extended consternation.

How decisions are made, and which ones are prioritized in order to move Christ's mission forward, influence the sense of "light" that the congregation as a whole will experience. When leadership decisions don't seem aligned or are not accompanied by enough explanation to clarify how this will further the church's kingdom purpose, debilitating clouds of our own creation form. What does it mean to serve in ministry leadership together and practice the Let There Be Light Breakthrough Prayer practice as you go? Here are a few suggestions.

After opening your meeting together with this particular breakthrough prayer practice, consider **organizing your agenda** according to the following format:

- Where do we see/have we seen God's clear "light" and need to act on it?

  These agenda items are ones where God's divine spotlight is hovering, and the ministry team or group has a sense that not to act would be procrastination. Move toward the light on these items by making decisions and action plans.

- Concerning what matters, questions, or possibilities are we experiencing "clouds"?

- Ask yourselves whether the "clouds" appear to block a path forward. If yes, take a moment to name the clouds. Do they exist around the actual situation(s), or are the clouds within any of us by our attitudes, fears, or resistance to change? Are the clouds a result of lack of communication, or information not shared between us? You may need to pause and pray for the guidance of the Spirit, and ask that you be shown Jesus—who is present in both our internal and external clouds.

- Once the clouds are named, identify steps that can be taken to move through the clouds and connect with Jesus's presence and direction. Will this call for courageous conversations, exploration of additional resources, or brainstorming new options? Or is it important to simply watch and wait for now?

- Do we see "shadows" anywhere in our agenda items where we don't quite have the clearness of details to feel confident moving ahead?

- Let the ministry team or group name what seems to be in the shadows and lacks clarity of detail. Are the shadows because we have not done the homework we need to prepare, so we lack the necessary information and preparation? Or is it a result of needing to consider different timing? Or is it something else?

- A next consideration is to reflect on this. Shadows obscure some of the landscape from our attention, so that what is lit and clear stands out. Given the shadows already named, what stands out in contrast? Is there an action step we are able to take, given the limited light we have?

An extra note belongs here about **lightning.** At times or in moments, a leader may have a flash of "light" or divine inspiration that gives a quick boost of focus or fuel to cloudy or shadowy situations or circumstances. I think of lightning moments as one type of answer to the Let There Be Light Breakthrough Prayer. As Psalm 97:1-2, 4 explains,

> *The Lord reigns, let the earth rejoice;*
> *Let the many islands be glad.*
> *Clouds and thick darkness surround Him . . .*
> *His lightnings lit up the world;*
> *The earth saw and trembled.* (NASB)

Using the Let There Be Light Breakthrough Prayer practice as a guide to your own role as a leader, and for your ministry team or group, results in a shift of perspective. It recasts the responsibilities and opportunities of your shared work, pulls you into a more foundational and ongoing life of prayer together as you seek God's light, and can fuel everyone's active spiritual growth. After all, if I discover that the "clouds" are within me—and that my clouds are holding back the service and progress of our ministry team—like Miriam in the previous story at Faith Church, I must accept the deep conviction and offer up willingness to receive the Spirit's transformation of my attitude, long-held opinions, fears, or defensiveness.

Finally, the most important evidence. You will notice when God's light is visibly separating the darkness in your congregation, and especially in you and your ministry team or group. It will be when the description found in 1 John 1:5-7 is actively being lived out. God's light within unites us without.

This is the message we have heard from Him and announce to you, that God is Light, and in Him there is no darkness at all. If we say that we have fellowship with Him and yet walk in the darkness, we lie and do not practice the truth; but if we walk in the Light as He Himself is in the Light, we have fellowship with one another. . . . (NASB)

Let There Be Light Prayer Handholds (Prayer-holds)

Begin the spiritual discipline of utilizing this breakthrough prayer practice as you look forward in faith. God is light, and the spiritual discipline of asking and looking for that light (as well as willingness to seek and find Jesus in any clouds) forms the anointed pathway of vital Christ followership. If additional prayer words or phrases might be useful prayer-holds for you, consider these possibilities, plus any others that inspire you.

Lampstand.

As Jesus conveyed to his followers, "*You are the light of the world. A city set on a hill cannot be hidden; nor does anyone light a lamp and put it under a basket, but on the lampstand, and it gives light to all who are in the house*" (Matthew 5:14-15 NASB). The prayer word lampstand could be a powerful refocus prayer for you on occasions when you are seeking courage to be a representative of God's light in a difficult setting and are asking God to allow that light to shine through you.

Armor of Light.

Paul wrote in Romans 13:12 about God's light actually providing spiritual protection. This prayer-hold is a request for God to help you wear the covering of Christ, the true light of the world, as you follow your faith.

Fruit of Light.

Have you ever noticed Paul reminded early church believers that the "*light [in Christ followers] produces fruit that consists of every sort of goodness, justice, and truth*" (Ephesians 5:9 CEB)? *Fruit of Light* may be a prayer-hold that invites God to enable you to reflect the light that you have seen.

Light and its dominant thematic presence throughout God's word may lead you, or you and your team, to additional study. The following scripture references can provide you a place to begin. How would you summarize light's role and impact as expressed in each of these? Is there a helpful prayer word or prayer-hold from any that seems to emerge for you?

- John 8:12

- Philippians 2:14-16

- Psalm 27:1

- Psalm 36:9

- Psalm 97:11

- Psalm 119:105

- Isaiah 9:2

- Luke 11:34-36

- John 1:1-4

- John 3:19-21

- Matthew 5:14-16

Discussion or Journal Questions for Application

Let There Be Light is a one-sentence breakthrough prayer practice that you can use in moments or seasons when you (and/or your team) are seeking clarity for God's best intention and priorities. Themes of light and darkness in scripture are descriptive of our own spiritual journey as we follow Christ, desiring to stay in God's light rather than get lost in darkness, stuck in the chaos of clouds, or turned around in the uncertainty that shadows create.

Do you wonder how to proceed or what to do next as you serve or lead? Do you ever feel completely "in the dark" about knowing how to handle an interaction with an unhappy church member? Or in your personal life, do you long for divine light to help you find your next steps? This breakthrough prayer practice invites the Holy Spirit not only to provide light around you, but also to shine light inside you to reveal what darkness needs to be transformed so you are receptive to the activity of the light.

You (or your team or congregation) may be in the grip of darkness, or have strongholds of brokenness, pain, or even habits that are holding you there. *Let There Be Light*—and may the True Light shine in your darkness.

Place a lit candle or other light in the center of your table or in a corner of the room. Acknowledge it as a symbol of God's ever-present light. (Consider the ongoing custom of placing a light or lit candle alongside your daily devotional time or to have present whenever your team or group meets.)

1. Which of the scriptures related to light and darkness named in this chapter spoke to you most significantly—and why? What particular impression or insight did God's Spirit bring you from it?

2. Where in the life of our church or in the work of our ministry team or group do you observe that we see clear "light" regarding God's priorities and direction? Are we acting on each of these, or are we holding off on any of them? If holding off, what clouds or shadows seem to block or distract us?

3. In your opinion, are the clouds or shadows you named positioned around our actual circumstances or challenges—or are any actually within us? If within, how would you describe what they might be?

4. Reflect on questions two and three on a personal level. What do you discover? Share with the group only what you are comfortable expressing.

5. If you as a team or group began to utilize the Let There Be Light Breakthrough Prayer practice, what would be the first shadowed or cloudy darkness upon which you would focus your prayer?

How about in your personal life?

As God responds, what evidence might you expect to see unfolding as light penetrates and clears your spiritual vision as a team? Personally?

6. Take a few moments to reflect back on any occasion you remember when God's light seemed to break through. Was it in a situation, a challenge, or inside you? What was the ripple of outplay when it happened? Did it involve any "lightning" moments for you or for anyone else? Give thanks for God's divine light as you share stories that give witness to the Almighty.

7. Discuss or journal the single-sentence or word version of a breakthrough prayer-hold practice that you would like to choose to add to your own ongoing spiritual disciplines. Is it *Let There Be Light*, or one of the prayer-holds listed in the chapter, or one you have otherwise identified that is directly relevant to any darkness, shadows, or clouds that you currently face?

Concluding Prayer Time

As a group, offer each person a turn that includes the following:

- Pray aloud the Let There Be Light Breakthrough Prayer that you intend to add to your daily practice in the season to come.

- If you are utilizing this as your team or group's resource, do a second go-around so that each person may also pray a specific Let There Be Light Prayer or word for your group's needs. Alternately, invite your team leader to do this on everyone's behalf.

QUICK-REMINDER SUMMARY #3

The third bead on my own breakthrough prayer practices strand I described in the introductory "Begin Here" chapter is from **Genesis 1:3-4: Let There Be Light**. This is the one-sentence breakthrough prayer that I pray when I find myself seeking light and clarity when surrounded by a sense of uncertainty-filled darkness. It's also the prayer when "clouds" or "shadows" appear, threatening to impair my ability to see and comprehend God's presence and priorities. I have also learned that this prayer, along with asking God to bring miraculous light around or before me, is a prayer asking God to shine the light of the Holy Spirit within me. The darkness, clouds, or shadows might actually be within my mind, attitude, and spirit in the form of emotions, unforgiveness, anger, brokenness, pride, judgmentalism, and more. God's purging light, to the extent I am willing to experience conviction and open myself to transformation, can remove forms of darkness in me that have kept me from seeing the leadership of Christ's light around me and have likely prevented me from reflecting the light of Christ to the world.

This third breakthrough prayer practice opens the door for God to remake my entire demeanor into the light-filled likeness of Christ within, so that I might recognize, follow, and join God's light-filled direction and work in the world.

Practice #4

"HOLY SURRENDER" BREAKTHROUGH PRAYER

Your kingdom come,
Your will be done,
On earth as it is in heaven.

—*Matthew 6:10 (NIV)*

WATCH #4 Holy Surrender Breakthrough Prayer Practice Video Story: Sarai

Find introductory videos featuring true stories that illustrate
the breakthrough prayer practice for each chapter of *Ultimate Reliance* at:
www.cokesbury.com/ultimate-reliance-study

One of the most significant milestones thus far in my life happened when a family member died following a lengthy cancer battle.

I remember myriad feelings and thoughts as I sat at the funeral service. The finality of it all, the realization that his former physical presence and entire earthly history was summarized now only by a few handfuls of ashes in an urn on the altar. I struggled to resign myself to the overwhelming irrevocability of it all. Our earthly relationship with him was over. A period had been placed at the end of our mutual sentence, with a hard stop.

Of course, I could have continued to try to live real-time ensconced in the memories and carry on with the behaviors appropriate to the previous reality. (In fact, I once became acquainted with a couple who lost their teenage son—and kept his bedroom untouched, just as he had left it, including his dirty laundry on the floor, for more than thirty years!) But living as though the past was still the present would have prevented my next season of life from taking root. As tempting as it was to cling to the familiarity of the past, I had to let go and give in. I had to release what had been in order to exchange it for an unknown but potential-filled next chapter of living. I would have to find the courage to face a new definition of my future without our family member. I would have to embrace trust and faith in order to change, grow, and mature into it, with God's loving guidance. The way toward wholeness was to release my attachment to what was, and to surrender to the new emptiness, the forward-facing space that it created within me. It would be within the new emptiness that God could and would create anew.

The funeral that day marked for me the end of what had been and opened for me what was to come. It was a milestone of inner spiritual decision: releasing a cherished past to say yes to an unknown future of significant proportion.

Not my will, but Thy will be done....

As I reflect back on following Jesus over time, there have been countless other occasions when I have sensed the Holy Spirit's urging to release some aspect of the present so that God could usher in a different future. Rather than having no alternative but to accept the loss of a loved one or other ending, my struggle far more frequently has been around my own choices to surrender various thoughts, desires, hopes, expectations, decisions and plans to which I've become attached.

I'm disappointed to say that selfishly I haven't always been willing to let go of a goal or picture in my mind, for example, or an assumption of what I think should happen or what I'm convinced a person around me should do—or what I have expected God should do. Sometimes it felt like a prayer of resignation to pray *Thy Will Be Done*, as though I were just giving up. Praying those words seemed on occasion like admitting I had failed on my own and now needed God to fix things (which, to be honest, often I did).

Praying *Thy Will Be Done* could even feel, well, lily-livered. Upon reflection, I realize now that those feelings emerged from a subconscious skepticism that maybe God couldn't or wouldn't really act if I released situations or decisions into those holy hands. With my lips I would speak words of confidence in God's miraculous will and work to others. But in my own prayers, evidently, I was suspicious that the Almighty was truly almighty. Praying *Thy Will Be Done* seemed like stepping off a steep cliff without a safety line, a craggy and lethal canyon far below, rather than stepping confidently forward with ears attuned to the beckoning words of Jesus: *"Come to Me, all you who are weary and heavy-laden, and I will give you rest"* (Matthew 11:28-30 NASB).

I have always longed for God's design—God's exquisite, mysterious handiwork throughout every moment and dimension of earthly daily living—in my life as a leader and in the congregations and teams I've led. Have you? Yet for that to happen, I've had to learn and then continue to form a proactive, healthier habit of this chapter's breakthrough prayer practice rather than falling back upon it like a last resort.

Holy Surrender—and a "White Funeral"

Jesus was completely clear with his disciples that praying for full, overall daily surrender to God's life and purpose, rather than their own, was to be central in their prayer lives. In fact, Jesus advised them thus:

"Pray, then, in this way:
'Our Father who is in heaven,
Hallowed be Your name.
'Your kingdom come.
Your will be done,
On earth as it is in heaven.'"
(Matthew 6:9-10 NASB)

Your will be done is what many refer to as "the prayer that never fails." Through prayer we bring ourselves or our situation to the supernatural threshold of God's love and grace, asking God to do what only God's wisdom and power is capable of doing. In this breakthrough prayer practice, we withhold attempting to give specific instructions, and instead place everything into God's amazing grace-filled grasp.

The original language that Jesus used as he taught his disciples what we now refer to as the Lord's Prayer reveals the potency of this prayer phrase. Rather than a tone of resigned resignation to the inscrutable will of God, "Your will be done" in its original New Testament Greek provides a more powerful nuance. "Will" may also be translated as "desire," revealing this as a prayer request for God's best. And the Greek verb usually translated into English as "be done" in most of our Bibles also could mean "to arise," "to appear in history," or "to break into

55

existence." Clearly, Jesus was urging his disciples to pray daily for God's preferred desires to miraculously emerge and be accomplished through our surrendered lives.

Jesus himself prayed this prayer three different times at the Garden of Gethsemane (Matthew 26:36-56), as he emptied himself of his own desires in order to surrender to God's eternal, history-changing intent. *Your will be done.* Rather than a prayer of just giving up or giving in, what a powerful breakthrough prayer of resurrection it truly is!

I refer to the breakthrough prayer practice of *Thy Will Be Done* as the Holy Surrender Prayer. By that I mean I am seeking release to the extent that I am indifferent to what the circumstances are or what the nature of the path is where God leads me, because my trust is fully complete that God is at work with God's best interests at heart. I have surrendered my own will for God's, and my trust and faith are so great that I am "indifferent" to God's choices for me. If you prefer, call this your "Holy Indifference" or "Holy Release" Breakthrough Prayer. The dictatorship of my own opinions, self-centered preferences, fears, ego, or brokenness are released—a "white funeral," as Oswald Chambers called it. I am wrapped only in the purpose of God's love, whatever form or shape that might take or where it might lead.

Oswald Chambers invented the term *white funeral* to define the ultimate spiritual wrestling match that results in our full surrender to God, based on Romans 6:4.

> No one enters into the experience of entire sanctification without going through a "white funeral"—the burial of the old life. If there has never been this crisis of death, sanctification is nothing more than a vision. There must be a "white funeral," a death that has only one resurrection—a resurrection into the life of Jesus Christ. Nothing can upset such a life; it is one with God for one purpose, to be a witness to Him. . . . We skirt the cemetery and all the time refuse to go to death. It is not striving to go to death, it is dying— "baptized into His death." (Oswald Chambers, *My Utmost for His Highest*, classic version, January 15 entry)

When surrendered prayer is difficult, it may be because vestiges of this wrestling match are still occurring around certain self-centered aspects of your old life that hold you back from God's fullest and best intent. You are "skirting the cemetery." You might not yet trust that God's will is preferable to your own. Or maybe you want to attempt to pick and choose which part of God's will to embrace. Or you want to desperately preserve without change that with which you have long been so comfortable (remember, as a literal illustration, the couple whose son's bedroom continued perpetually untouched).

Personal preferences and longtime entrenched perspectives are both ingredients that are capable of interfering with a beautiful "white funeral" outplay of God's preferred design. "Skirting the cemetery" can happen in the life of a leader, within a leadership team, or even across an entire congregation without anyone realizing it. Let's take a closer look.

Holy Surrender: Ministry Leadership

Pastor Camille had always worked to be proactive in every congregation she led. Her leaders at Oak Street Church had obliged her request that a "vision planning retreat" happen within a few months of her arrival as their new pastor, so that they could organize and strategize for a new season. Her finance committee was conscientious to help keep the church's spending within its conservative budget, especially when it came to ministry expenses. Worship services ran on time, and the choir had a well-trained director who coordinated song choices with the sermon theme each week. A long-standing hospitality team always staffed the church lobby, providing a friendly greeting to newcomers and offering them a coffee mug emblazoned with the church name on it as a welcome gift. The annual pancake feed, "Trunk or Treat" for children in late October, and the Christmas bake sale were historically well attended. And now Pastor Camille was eager to kick off a new church-wide Breakthrough Prayer Initiative. After all, the decade-long slow decline in which Oak Street Church had found itself needed to be reversed. Now was the time to move the church into praying for God to bring new hopes and dreams for their future together. The time was ripe to surrender and trust God for new possibilities to come.

Camille got the initial step of the Breakthrough Prayer Initiative launched just after the first of the new year. She took her administrative council to silently prayer-walk the sanctuary during the first ten minutes of their meeting time, asking God to break through anew in the persons who would attend worship the coming Sunday, in the work of the council itself, and in the congregation as a whole.

When the administrative council returned to its meeting room afterward, Pastor Camille announced that they would begin all council meetings throughout the year with ten minutes of prayer-walking together. They would saturate different areas of their church facility with prayers, asking God to bring new hopes and dreams for the congregation.

She was eager to find out what the new prayer-walking experience had felt like for them. Several murmured positive affirmations. Then John, the longtime church trustee chair who was typically a man of few words other than his monthly report on repairs of the building, unexpectedly spoke up.

"Prayer doesn't work for me," he confessed, looking down. "I only went on that breakthrough prayer walk because you told us to come with you, and because it was the first agenda item printed on the list for tonight's meeting. But to be honest, I have never seen God do even one thing I've prayed for, and I haven't ever bothered God unless it's something big. But God just ignores me, has always ignored me, and doesn't do anything. Same for this church actually. Nothing big we've ever prayed for has happened. So I don't pray anymore. I just try to tolerate the people around me who keep giving it a try. I guess you all may still be thinking you can get God's ear one of these days. But I don't think it will ever happen."

A few council members shifted uneasily. No one spoke. As the silence grew, most looked instinctively at Pastor Camille to see her reaction.

"John, I'm sorry to hear your experience with prayer has not been positive over the long haul. What were some of the prayers that God seemed to ignore, or said no? Do you feel comfortable telling us more? There may be others in the room who share your perspective, and it would be a valuable discussion for all of us if you could say more."

John shook his head, collecting himself. Then, after several moments, he began to speak haltingly.

"Well, one of the biggest was about twenty years ago. I remember because I was the new trustee chair, just a few years into holding this position. We needed money for a roof repair and didn't have it. So we all prayed that God would give us the money for it. But God didn't. I remember being very angry at God, and I wasn't alone. We all realized God was just ignoring our prayers, as usual. It was a big crisis. The roof began to leak, and then with one big thunderstorm we had a flood down on the south wing hallway of the building. Ruined everything. And we were all praying…and God didn't do a thing. We even prayed asking for the thunderstorm to stop, and God said no to that. Prayer just doesn't matter."

"That sounds like it must have brought quite a crisis to the congregation. What ended up happening?" Pastor Camille inquired.

"Well, the pastor we had at the time didn't like talking about money with church members. But we told him he was going to have to change his attitude and take some responsibility—the church building looked like a disaster area. It was quite a fight, and voices were raised. Finally, the pastor told us that we would have to join him in talking to church members about money as well. If he had to do it, the council had to do it also. So we split up the membership list, and each of us took some names. And we gave ourselves two weeks to go talk to the people on our list about how we were going to have to raise the money to fix the roof and get professional help for the cleanup. We were begging our people, I tell you. It was terrible. When it was all said and done, people ended up kicking in enough not only to fix the roof, but also for the cleanup and even new carpeting in the hallways of both wings. But we did it ourselves. And that pastor ended up leaving; he was so angry that we told him he needed to help raise the money. That's how the church works. We have to do everything. Not God."

Madelyn, the women's ministry committee chair, interrupted. "Well, now with John reminding us of that, I can also remember just a few years ago when this council prayed specifically, and God also didn't provide. Praying got everyone's hopes up, and then when God didn't open the door we felt very let down, became suspicious about praying for anything, and promised ourselves we wouldn't get the congregation's hopes up again about praying like that. It kinda soured some of us on prayer beyond the ones we read from the book of liturgy in worship on Sundays, which are safe enough. Does anyone remember back when we were all praying about a grant from our denomination? It was about two years before Pastor Camille came, and it would have allowed us to finally have the money to hire a youth director onto our staff. Adding a youth staff person was a long-held dream here, and still is. But God shut that door with a loud no because we obviously didn't get the grant. So we were forced to figure out something different as a stopgap. We ended up having to scramble to find volunteers from the congregation to just keep the youth group going."

Camille couldn't hold back. "But one of the biggest reasons I felt led to accept the call to serve as your pastor was actually because of your youth ministry. It's completely led by the most gifted volunteer leaders I've ever seen! We have the largest youth ministry in our town, with teens bringing their friends who don't have a church home to hear about a relationship with Christ. I would call it our most significant outreach we have going on across our entire church. Just last Wednesday night, this building was filled to overflowing with middle- and high-school students. And there must have been at least fifteen adults here as the youth ministry leadership team."

"Yes," Madelyn affirmed sadly. "Isn't it too bad that those church members are having to give up so much time to take care of the youth group every week? If only God would have blessed us with that grant, we would have a paid youth director to take care of all that work. I think John may be more right than we realize about the times we've prayed, and God has not given us what we wanted or seemed to say no. We have just had to figure out what to do on our own, since God didn't provide what we prayed for so earnestly—or even respond. We had put the grant for a youth director on the prayer chain and everything. Lots of people prayed for that grant, but we got absolutely nothing as a result."

Camille fingered the page before her on the table, which was the council's meeting agenda for the evening. She prayed a silent inner prayer for guidance and felt the Holy Spirit's leading to take the meeting in a different direction with additional discussion about the specific Holy Surrender Breakthrough Prayer practice. Could it be that her administrative council—and maybe even the congregation—had been so focused on what they were instructing God to do for them that they missed noticing what miraculous breakthroughs had happened?

"You know, friends, I am so thankful that John has opened up our conversation about the power of prayer. And it sounds like some of us have questions about whether prayer actually does have 'power'—and if so, how much. Am I right?" A few heads nodded in agreement.

"Right now I am flooded with a memory of my own. May I share a personal story? All through growing up, I had dreamed of becoming a research physician. I told everyone I would go to medical school one day. In the speech I gave as valedictorian on the day I graduated from high school, I even proclaimed that I would eventually discover a cure for cancer so lives could be saved. Then I went on to the university. After taking the basic required courses, I enrolled in biochemistry, advanced biology, and anatomy. But I struggled to handle those advanced classes, let alone excel in them. It became painfully clear by my junior year of college that despite the tutors I was working with, the extra help I was receiving from my instructors, and all the hours I was investing in studying, God wasn't going to grant me my chosen life dream. Even though I had been praying more for God's help than ever before in my life, I was barely passing the very college prep courses I needed.

"I participated in a college students' Bible study at that time. I remember one week after everyone else had left, I poured out my bitterness, anger, embarrassment, and disappointment to the group leader. She had a kind and sympathetic ear. I ranted and raged at God's refusal to give me the aptitude required to fulfill my longtime dream, despite all my prayers pleading for it. Finally, my energy was spent, and I began to sob. She held my hand as I let the emotions out. When I could speak, I heard myself saying, 'So what should I do next? I have no future. I am terrified. What should I do with my life now? My one central goal is clearly not to be, and I'm so humiliated. I feel like God has abandoned me. Prayer is just wishful thinking after all!'

Long story short, in my most miserable life disappointment, that Bible study leader wrote me a letter a few days later. It was a letter that changed my entire faith life relative to prayer. I kept the handwritten original in my Bible for a long time, and when it became dog-eared, I made a photocopy of it that I carry still. In fact, I wonder if I can pull it out read it to you now? It seems like just the right moment."

Camille pulled the letter from her Bible and began to read.

Dear Camille,

Thank you for sharing with me after Bible study. I have pondered your struggle with prayer and thought it might be most useful for your consideration if I wrote you this note with my thoughts on paper.

Here's what I've learned about prayer. God doesn't give us what we ask for with our ideas or wishes. *God gives us what we allow through our surrender.* Remember Jesus praying at the Garden of Gethsemane? He was willing for the death of his own preference so that God's greater preference could go forward. *"Not what I want, Lord, but what You want...."*

You see, the primary purpose of prayer isn't to get God to do things for us, protect us, or to shower us with special blessings and gifts—although God does love to do that at times.

The real purpose of prayer is to surrender ourselves for God to do things in and through us.

As long as you and I have a long list of requirements and "givens" or parameters for what we insist God must work within or accomplish on our behalf, we will always be disappointed in the journey of prayer. Yes, as difficult as it is right now, that also includes your unsuccessful attempt to require God to grant your medical school dream. But how about this perspective: maybe your "failure" is actually, in God's eyes, "success" in progress.

Do you really believe prayer makes a difference, and that a divine response begins to happen the moment that you pray? If so, it transforms the death of a dream into a positive road sign steering you toward what is God's "yes" for your life instead. Rather than feeling disappointed when God says "no" to a dream or request, what if we got excited that God provided the "no" as a forward stepping-stone so that we could continue to stay moving and surrendered to discovering God's far better ideas instead?

Everything of our own making—

> our subconscious suspicions that somehow God won't or isn't capable of doing beyond what we could ask, think or imagine;

> our lofty ambitions of importance in the eyes of others, or desire for material gain;

> our resistance to or fear of change and the subsequent spiritual transformation that surrender would invoke;

> and our refusal to traverse a strange, unexpected path that's not of our own choosing

—any and all of this hinders our awareness and openness to the extraordinary efficacy of prayer.

Now that you have surrendered the life dream of your own making, let's be expectant as you pray, as Jesus did, *Your Will Be Done.* I am praying along with you. Adventures of God's creation for a new life dream await!

The council sat quietly when Pastor Camille finished reading, refolded the photocopied letter, placed it back in her Bible, and then spoke.

"I could have never, ever imagined that God would answer my prayer begging to discover a cure for cancer by leading me to become a pastor and spend my life instead helping people discover the eternal 'cure' found in Jesus! I finally realized that trying to insist I knew best how God should answer my prayer led only to my own disappointment. It wasn't until I surrendered my own demands of how God should accomplish my dreams that God had room to break through with the best versions of those dreams."

Then she asked, "Is there any other angle we should consider on how God may have actually answered your prayers here at Oak Street Church?"

"For a youth director, you mean?" Madelyn corrected her. "That's what we prayed for, the money we needed. And it didn't happen."

Camille smiled. "Yes, I heard you say that the church's prayers were specifically for money to pay a youth director. And when the grant wasn't awarded, you concluded God failed you. But what if you had surrendered your insistence to God that the only way wonderful youth ministry could happen would be through a paid staff person? Wasn't your real bottom-line desire for fruitful, effective youth ministry to flourish here at Oak Street Church? God must have loved that heartfelt desire, which was actually behind the prayers for the grant, right? Look how God has abundantly answered, and the many talented and passionate youth ministry volunteers who are serving out of their gifts!"

Then once again John spoke up. This time his emotions were evident.

"Well, that might be true about what God did through our church prayers about youth ministry. And now you are probably going to point out that God provided the money for the roof through all the work we put into individually asking a whole lot of very reluctant people to donate. But it actually brought out the very worst in our members that they took out on the council. The council had to split up the membership list and go tell everyone that either they had to chip in money or else our damaged building might be condemned by the city. We had doors slammed in our faces by members who left to attend other churches, and we were criticized for talking as much as we had to in the worship services about getting people to step up and give. You can't call that the hand of God. It was way too ugly of a season in our congregation."

Pastor Camille's voice was gentle. "John, it's possible for an entire congregation to collectively struggle, just as I did individually, with exchanging our own willful, selfish preferences for God's more excellent way. I can imagine that if the congregation had never really been taught and discipled that a life of faith always includes godly stewardship of financial and material resources, it would have felt like a distasteful intrusion to them for you all to have insisted that they prioritize investing additional money in the church's emergency building needs."

"Are you saying our church members aren't good Christians?" asked Madelyn defensively. "We have wonderful people here, most of whom show up every Sunday. We have dozens of them who purchase a poinsettia every Advent season to be placed on the altar in memory or in honor of someone. And most don't even take their poinsettias home after the Christmas Eve services, which allows us to donate them to the retirement center residents a few blocks away. That clearly shows how generous our members are."

"Agreed, they are very thoughtful in that manner. What I want to make clear is that a hallmark of spiritual maturity is not only giving what is extra that we don't really need ourselves. It's also sharing what God has given us, with a cheerful heart and also sacrificially when we need to—like when the church building sustained the damage. Practicing the Holy Surrender Breakthrough Prayer gradually trains us to remove our will so that it can be replaced with God's desires, even if it means using our money differently than we had wanted. Or using our time differently than we had wanted, which is what the outstanding volunteer team is doing with evident joy as they serve the needs of the youth ministry. Yes, sometimes the Holy Surrender Prayer practice causes us to wrestle with God. And the outcome could look different than what we might have thought we wanted. But guess who always wins—thank goodness—?" Camille smiled as she looked around the room.

A faint but discernable flicker of a smile crossed John's face. He shook his head, then suddenly raised his hand and leaned across the table to give a high five to a surprised Pastor Camille. "I've got to hand it to you, Pastor. It's probably a good thing you didn't turn out to be a doctor. You really do believe prayer makes a difference, don't you! Well, maybe that breakthrough prayer walk you took us on at the start of this meeting worked after all. Maybe I was wrong, what I said about it. It seems to me like this meeting itself has had a couple of breakthroughs. Looks like you've begun to get us seeing that prayer makes a difference a little more as well, when we look at it from God's perspective. Let's all say 'Amen.'"

You—Together with Ministry Traveling Companions

When my family member died, I was forced to surrender my dreams of what was once for what was to come, whether I liked it or not. However, far more often, the spiritual journey of the Holy Surrender Breakthrough Prayer practice is *choosing* to surrender my will, or our will as a ministry team, in order to allow room for God's. Both personally and as a leader, I've found it helpful to make a reminder list of what stumbling blocks can result in an individual's or group's resistance to full surrender. Certain factors pull us in the opposite direction of surrender, so let's pray and live aware of them. Otherwise, they create spiritual detours that can be destructive and painful to the accomplishment of God's desires in and through us personally or as leaders of our church or ministry.

Consider the following both individually and then together with your group, and ask yourselves whether any stumbling blocks are hindering or helping your ultimate reliance on God's faithfulness and supernatural resources.

1. *Falling into the assumption that prayer's primary purpose is for God to bless or provide what we want*—rather than to become surrendered to what God wants.

2. *Getting others to pity us that God hasn't done what we asked.* Remember, when we are truly following Jesus we cannot be pitiful and powerful at the same time.

3. *Having misgivings that come because our human minds are unable to figure out how God could possibly respond to the matter about which we are praying.* Because we can't resolve or find a pathway through ourselves, we might spend endless, unproductive time in meetings attempting to imagine or speculate how God might be able to. The fact is, however, that when we surrender in prayer, the resourcing comes from above rather than from within our human selves. Isn't that what the woman at the well learned from Jesus? (Check out the story in John 4:4-42.)

4. *Only praying about one option.* As long as we are praying specifically for only one single option, we may be closing

ourselves off to spiritual flexibility for God to lead us according to God's greater wisdom. Unless God has led everyone to pray about just a single possibility, it may become more empowering in prayer to ask God's Spirit to show various paths or choices as you pray through to surrender. This might more readily help us release our own demands, requirements, and nonnegotiables, and it could also open hearts and shift any complaining attitude ("God isn't listening to what we are specifically asking for!") to a bigger landscape of God's miraculous intent that is likely at play.

5. *Not including the Holy Surrender Breakthrough Prayer every time you pray.* This breakthrough prayer practice trains spiritual nimbleness and responsiveness into you, brings your spiritual eyes increasing acuity to look up and out for where and how God may be leading, and keeps you spiritually yielded enough to step out and follow. Do not mistakenly assume that you will automatically have courage to act when a new breakthrough opportunity opens up if you haven't been practicing the Holy Surrender breakthrough prayer. Otherwise, reactions might include "But that would mean..." and "But I would have to give up this/that..." and "I'm not ready...." Doubt or skepticism might spring up like weeds in a newly planted garden. Nothing will have the power to stop you from living into God's answers to your prayers, however, if you have already habitually been practicing full surrender daily in your prayer life. After all, when Jesus taught his closest disciples how to pray daily (Matthew 6), he included the Holy Surrender Prayer for them.

6. *Not noticing the emotions that may accompany the process of Holy Surrender, and then releasing them to flow past.* We are all entitled to our feelings. But stoking the fires of a sense of loss, sadness that our desires were not God's, our anger, disappointment, or resentment will only hold back holistic, potential-laden surrender to the Almighty.

7. *Not accepting that God's timeframe is not always our time-frame.* Who knows? God's full response may be hindered time-wise due to your unwillingness to surrender hate,

brokenness, judgmentalism, self-defeating habits, negative self-talk, poor self-care, or insistence upon your own desires. Or it may be affected by the level of readiness of others who will be impacted. Regular practice of the Holy Surrender Breakthrough Prayer brings opportunity for your own transformation, preparation, and maturity of faith. (You'll find even more about this in Chapter 5 with the Pickaxe Breakthrough Prayer practice.)

8. *Losing sight of what the Holy Surrender Prayer is NOT.* It is not tolerating abuse or evil, or co-signing sinful, destructive behavior of others around you. By praying "Thy Will Be Done," we surrender ourselves to being available to stand up and speak up when God's Spirit prompts us, or to exit from such actions or environments.

Holy Surrender Prayer Handholds (Prayer-holds)

As you begin the regular spiritual discipline of utilizing this particular breakthrough prayer practice, you may gradually begin to notice how much you are holding onto in mind and heart—memories, unforgiveness, certain attitudes, a sense of entitlement, or even rules by which you believe God should or must always act.

Use the Holy Surrender Prayer or other prayer-holds to help yourself surrender more fully to the Creator of the universe, the One who sent his only Son into the world so that we might experience the same resurrected new eternal life through Christ within ourselves. It is only by releasing that which blocks our ability to recognize and respond to God's movement and activity, by living into a "white funeral" instead of "skirting the cemetery," that we can experience ongoing breakthroughs of new life and hope.

Try out any of these prayer words, or prayer-holds, throughout your day to help train yourself in the Holy Surrender Breakthrough Prayer practice.

Gift.

Throughout the history of Christianity, spiritual leaders have written and spoken of a prayer lifestyle that views anything and everything as a gift that has the Spirit-leveraged potential to bless, refine, guide, prune, and shape us. Using this prayer word as you navigate daily living can keep this lens on your spiritual eyes regarding whatever unfolds as containing potential benefit.

Hold close the message from Jesus found in Luke 11:11-13:

Now suppose one of you fathers is asked by his son for a fish; he will not give him a snake instead of a fish, will he? Or if he is asked for an egg, he will not give him a scorpion, will he? If you then, being evil, know how to give good gifts to your children, how much more will your heavenly Father give the Holy Spirit to those who ask Him? (NASB)

Sweep.

Like the story Jesus told of sweeping a home clean of evil spirits, so Holy Surrender Breakthrough Prayer practice accomplishes the inner sweeping clean of your mind, heart, and spirit of any selfish desires or poor attitudes in order to make yourself wide open and available for that which is far better.

Take a look at Luke 11:24-26, and the warning Jesus made about keeping the house of your life swept and in order, which this breakthrough prayer practice will help you do.

When an unclean spirit leaves a person, it wanders through dry places looking for a place to rest. But it doesn't find any. Then it says, "I'll go back to the house I left." When it arrives, it finds the house cleaned up and decorated. Then it goes and brings with it seven other spirits more evil than itself. They go in and make their home there. That person is worse off at the end than at the beginning. (CEB)

Release.

The use of this one-word prayer-hold may gently guide you along as you grow in your longing to trade your own yearning for God's intentional will—even in times when you do not prefer what is clearly God's path ahead.

Jesus taught his disciples to pray that God's will would be done, and he prayed it multiple times in surrender just prior to his arrest and eventual crucifixion. As he hung on the cross, even Jesus struggled, wondering aloud if he had been given a snake instead of a fish (*"My God, my God, why have you forsaken me?"*). Yet, with a loud cry, he surrendered and "released his spirit" (Matthew 27:45-50) to receive a gift beyond comprehension on behalf of the redemption of the world.

Discussion or Journal Questions for Application

Thy Will Be Done is the fourth one-sentence breakthrough prayer practice that you can use in moments or seasons when you (and/or your team) are seeking to remove your will so that God's will can be done. Use the following questions in your own journal and reflection time, or together with your team or group, as steps toward enhancing your leadership of holy surrender.

Begin your time by using one of the prayer-holds named above (or one of your own choosing), each person naming it aloud around your circle (or individually). Then allow a time of silent prayer, as each person releases other mental agenda items or distractions to allow inner quiet and peace for spiritual listening. Conclude the silent prayer time by all saying together, "Thy Will Be Done. Amen."

Respond to the following journal/reflection/discussion questions as appropriate to your setting, individually and collectively.

1. Do you remember a time in the life of our congregation, or in your own life, when we (or you) clearly chose to surrender to God in a situation, matter, or decision? If so, name this time. How did you feel? What was the eventual outplay?

2. How about a time or occasion when we as a church (or you individually) didn't choose but were instead forced or presented with a situation or circumstance that you had to surrender and accept? Name this situation or circumstance and describe your feelings at the time.

3. Do you believe we (or you) were able to release the disappointment or other reactions in order for God to weave through a greater divine good? Why or why not, and what has been the outcome? Mention whether you believe that additional surrender is still needed around the situation or circumstance you named, and what might be holding you back.

4. Look again at the story of Pastor Camille and her council. What do you think had initially held them back from embracing "Thy Will Be Done" from a more fruitful perspective? What could have been handled differently? Are there any insights from the story to learn and apply to your own congregational leadership, or in your own life?

5. Review this chapter's list of eight ingredients that might pull us (or you) off your commitment to holy surrender. Which of these might our team have experienced as we accomplish our work and service together? Have we ever been guilty of "skirting the cemetery" rather than yielding up our own comfortable preferences in order to open ourselves to God's intent?

Concluding Prayer Time

- If you have one, provide for the group's use (or your own) a palm-sized prayer gripping cross. Pass it around from one to the next person. Each person is invited to hold the prayer gripping cross as a "white funeral" symbol, and name aloud (or silently) a need, situation, circumstance, or challenge to offer to God's breakthroughs that you intend to continue to surrender ongoing in your prayer practice.

- Alternately, invite your team leader to do this on everyone's behalf, if during your discussion a primary situation, need, or circumstance to surrender to God has collectively emerged.

- - - - - - - - - - - - - - - - - - - -

QUICK-REMINDER SUMMARY #4

The fourth bead on my own breakthrough prayer practices strand I described in the introductory "Begin Here" chapter is from **Matthew 6:10: Thy Will Be Done.** This is the one-sentence breakthrough prayer that I pray daily to help keep myself surrendered and open to God's preferred dreams and possibilities, rather than stubbornly demand my own. It is only by releasing my preferences, requirements, and convictions of what I think I will or will not do or let happen that I become spiritually agile enough to respond to God's leading. And the ongoing breakthrough prayer practice of *Thy Will Be Done* also increases my spiritual acuity to recognize God's activity and desires. The Holy Surrender Prayer is not one of resignation, defeat, or failure. Rather, it is prayerfully sweeping my inner spiritual room clean so that God has space for ongoing makeovers of breakthrough proportions.

- - - - - - - - - - - - - - - - - - -

"PICKAXE" BREAKTHROUGH PRAYER

Keep on asking,
and you will receive what you ask for.
Keep on seeking,
and you will find.
Keep on knocking,
and the door will be opened to you.

—Matthew 7:7 (NLT)

WATCH #5 Breakthrough Prayer Practice Video Story: Forest Chapel Church

Find introductory videos featuring true stories that illustrate
the breakthrough prayer practice for each chapter of *Ultimate Reliance* at:
www.cokesbury.com/ultimate-reliance-study

As a small child I remember sitting at the breakfast table on warm summer mornings, with the windows open to let the ceaseless breeze of the Kansas plains meander through. Part of the memories embedded deep from those young years was the incessant *rat-a-tat-tat* of a woodpecker who lived in a tree just outside our house. I remember marveling at the tenacity as he seemed to hammer away diligently for extended periods of time. I used to wonder when and how he knew that his job was complete, and even what he was trying to accomplish. But the exemplary focused diligence he provided was impressive. And though I never once caught a glimpse of the woodpecker visually, the sound of his inspiration to stick with it and do whatever it took—for as long as it took—remains with me to this day.

As I grew up, I soon learned that we humans have long attempted to replicate this bird's strategy with a tool designed to accomplish similar tightly-targeted tasks. In fact, the name for the tool we've long referred to as a "pickaxe" originally evolved from the medieval Latin word for woodpecker. History describes a pickaxe as having been useful for farming, mining, and even in battle. Just like the hammering of a pointed beak against a tree trunk, the repeated swing of a pickaxe today can break up rock or sod in your garden when leveraged with enough ongoing tenacity to eventually break through.

If the description of the woodpecker's audible "artillery fire" among the tree branches awakens a sense of recognition to you—or if you've ever repeatedly swung a real pickaxe yourself—you've captured the spirit of the breakthrough prayer practice I refer to as Pickaxe Prayer. This fifth prayer practice is the style Jesus described to listeners as part of his historic Sermon on the Mount, proclaimed on the shore of Lake Galilee.

Jesus emphasized the importance of ongoing prayer as a ceaseless praxis: bringing before God those situations or requests in which you long for God to act, to respond, and to transform. Did Jesus have multiple specific intentions for recommending that we "ask, seek, knock" in prayer, as noted in Matthew 7:7? Let's look closer.

In the original Greek language of Jesus's day, the word he used that we translate as *ask* was actually a verb often reserved to describe a servant, worker, or slave's urgent begging of the master. It indicated a heartfelt craving or desire expressed by someone lesser to someone greater or more powerful. And the present imperative tense Jesus used, which more accurately could be translated as "keep asking," paints a picture that our prayer requests to the great God of all resources should become an ongoing, active habit.

When Jesus stated his instructions that our prayer requests should become a practice, he then named the importance of a second step: to *keep seeking*. Also in present imperative tense, the original Greek for this verb had a rich connotation. Its broad essence includes thoughtful and careful consideration, deliberation, investigation, or active endeavors. This is the same word Jesus used in the parable found in Matthew 13:45 as he described a merchant seeking fine pearls, and also the parable of a woman searching carefully for her precious lost coin (Luke 15:8).

Could it be that Jesus was urging us to develop our prayer lives to become more than simply begging God for whatever crosses our minds? Was he instructing us to be mindful of our investment of reflection, observation, and proactive willingness to explore new options alongside those prayers, which would then create more room for God's responses to be birthed?

After all, the Greek word for *find* that Jesus used is also translated elsewhere as "to discover," "to hit upon," "to learn," "to detect," or "to recognize." Perhaps Jesus wanted us to understand that persistent breakthrough prayer accompanied by our own active, careful, Spirit-guided quest may open our eyes anew to the divine's leading or provision. More importantly, God may need to change or transform our own perspective, behavior, attitude, or mindset in order to see and participate in the Spirit's response that's unfolding.

Jesus rounded out his teaching about how to pray by advising his listeners to *keep knocking.* Your knuckles knock on the hard surface of a closed door, which is necessary in order to receive a response. Both Jesus's Greek and our English translation of this verb alike make clear that he was comparing the practice of prayer to rapping or thumping against something that has an initial resistance.

Even more graphic, the particular Greek word Jesus utilized for "open" in this verse—as a result of knocking—literally meant "to break," "to open," or "to make possible." What relevance this brings as a literal breakthrough prayer practice description straight from Jesus himself! Elsewhere in the New Testament, the same Greek verb was used to describe the heavens opening and the Holy Spirit descending like a dove at the time of Jesus's baptism (Matthew 3:16); a deaf man's ears miraculously opening when Jesus healed him (Mark 7:35); and many other amazing moments that could not have unfolded other than by an opening initiated by the Almighty.

To summarize, then, the depiction that Jesus's listeners heard that day about the practice and purpose of prayer was that

- it requires a ready willingness to keep placing our needs and requests for breakthroughs and new possibilities before God;

- it includes inner reflection, deliberation, and meditation so that the Holy Spirit can transform us in order to reveal discernment;

- it calls for a bold, faith-filled persistence to pray in the face of seeming resistance, repeatedly and ongoing like the woodpecker hammering on a tree trunk, with confidence and trust that supernaturally designed, eventual breakthroughs of God's new possibilities will open.

Matthew 7:7 is *not* Jesus's provision of a simple, magic-like prayer formula that functions as a silver bullet or a blank check, practically guaranteeing that whatever the pray-er asks and desires will automatically be granted. Rather, we gain another breakthrough prayer practice that is multidimensional. It requires tireless prayer, a heart of increasing faith-filled commitment, and an ongoing walk of faith following the Master. Or, as this anonymous quote summarizes,

Tenacity is essential to power in prayer:
the life must knock
while the lips ask
and the heart seeks.

This Pickaxe Breakthrough Prayer practice underscores the value of proactively continuing to pray for breakthroughs even when there's a resistant closed door. Maybe you have given up hope and prayer when a "door" seems impossibly locked shut. If you have, avoid lapsing into a cynical, fatalistic, nonscriptural skepticism that somehow prayer doesn't matter, and that "God will do what God will do anyway." What a far cry that is from this active, persistent, hope-filled prayer practice Jesus outlined.

Pickaxe Breakthrough Prayer: Ministry Leadership

Pastor Luke felt at the top of his game as he completed the last year at seminary, preparing to move into pastoring a church. He had gotten outstanding grades in preaching class, had taken advantage of a knack for learning languages in the master of divinity Greek and Hebrew exegetical courses, and kept himself in the same fit, excellent picture of health and vitality as developed back in high school when he had been the star quarterback. In fact, Luke was confident that his denominational judicatory would appoint him right out of school into a large, prominent congregation, despite his limited clergy experience. With his scholastic record and history of various achievements, he spoke with confidence to others about his lofty ministry career expectations. Every morning in his devotional time, he included prayers for God's preparation and direction for the next chapter of his vocational calling. Yet, as graduation day gradually approached, no word about his first church appointment came. Finally his phone rang just two days before seminary would be finished, with the long-awaited news.

"Luke, we have finally identified the right first pastoral appointment for you," the district superintendent's voice announced. "It's a three-quarter-time clergy position at Trinity Church, which sits just on the edge of Maple County. It's perfect for someone like you who's right out of school. We believe that with careful leadership, you will disciple the people into financial generosity that will increase the church's income and budget so that you can eventually be paid for full time. But that will be up to you and your diligence to grow generous givers. Actually, it is amazing that they have agreed to pay you three-quarter time, since right now the worship attendance has been averaging around thirty people or so. It's a church in decline, mostly older folks. But of course, with your leadership all that can change. There are mostly elderly members, and a few of them are the ones primarily underwriting the budget right now."

Luke felt emotions rising inside as his mind raced. Maple County was in the most rural area of the state. Only a couple of small population centers, each containing a few hundred people plus a grocery store and gas station, could be found anywhere in the miles of farmland, dotted with tiny communities of a few dozen houses among the acres of crops and cattle. With his obvious gifts and talents, plus his stellar GPA as he prepared to graduate with top honors, was this the best clergy placement the judicatory officers of his denomination could provide?

"There must be a major mistake here," he heard himself attempting to counter the district superintendent as clearly as he could. "Why would you put someone like me way out there in the middle of nowhere? I mean, I assume I am at the top of your list of new ministers coming into our system. I'm ready and primed for a setting in the suburbs, where new houses are being built and young families are moving in. Or else one of our denomination's big historic churches in the city, filled with key civic leaders and executives. I think I would at least make an excellent associate pastor for one of those, bring bench depth with my preaching and all the rest...."

"Nope, no mistake, Luke. Trinity Church in Maple County will be your first appointment."

"Well, I refuse. My answer is no! I have worked too hard to be stuck someplace like that right out of school. That's not what I want, not what I have worked so hard to prepare for, and it's not a good fit for me!" Luke was almost shouting now. He struggled to restrain his hot anger, disappointment, and outrage at the insult of this placement. How would he face his fellow classmates and admit he was being appointed to what was likely a remotely located, dying church with just a few members still hanging on?

There was a long silence on the other end of the phone. Then, the calm voice finally replied with a clear note of finality. "Luke, you appeared before our clergy credentialing board last January and pledged that you would serve and lead God's church wherever you were placed once you graduated. Unless you wish to now exit our denomination's clergy ranks, this is your appointment. I would like to set up a meeting with you and the church leaders out on location at Trinity Church this Sunday, the day after graduation, in order to introduce you to them. Would three in the afternoon work for you to be there? You'll be able to walk through the church building that day and also take a look at the parsonage, which is just on the other side of the church's gravel drive. I believe they replaced the carpet in the living room in preparation for their next pastor."

Luke struggled all that week in his morning devotional time and prayer. It all felt like he was living out a bad movie. Luke finally decided to keep praying that something else, a different opportunity, would suddenly open up. Yes, that was it. He would keep praying, keep hammering away at God to somehow deliver him from this dead end of an appointment and get him to where he rightfully belonged: leading a congregation that appreciated his gifts and could advantage them best. God was certainly capable of a miracle, and Luke would just keep asking for one. Isn't that what Jesus taught everyone to do?

Pastor Luke was sullen as he was introduced Sunday afternoon to Alice and Harry, the chair and vice chair of the Trinity Church council. Alice, who had just turned ninety-one years old, politely told Luke she had been born into the Trinity congregation and that her parents had been founding members. Harry was a retired farmer in his eighties who also handled the church treasurer responsibilities. Harry recounted proudly the history of how he and several other members had built the tiny parsonage piecemeal themselves four decades earlier on the church property. The living room carpet had indeed just been replaced, Harry explained. They had thought that after thirty-plus years, it was probably time.

Luke asked to look inside the small Trinity Church building. It was like a quaint miniature rectangular box, with a classic white steeple on top. Old, chipped stained-glass windows adorned the front wall of the sanctuary just behind the altar area, and the afternoon sunlight filtered through to reveal the scuffs and stains on its hardwood floor. Outdated and well-worn hymnals were stacked neatly at the end of each pew. "The organ in here hasn't worked for years," Alice admitted apologetically. "We just use the piano in the corner instead. It originally belonged to Mildred Shepler and was donated to the church by her family when she passed a while back. Her daughter now plays it for service on Sundays."

Luke experienced his long-held expectation of leading a church that featured worship with a talented, contemporary worship and praise band vaporizing instantly, right along with everything else he had always anticipated having at his disposal when he finally got to lead his own church. He felt empty, and tried to rally himself to pray in his spirit as part of his commitment to keep asking God over and over again for something different. But he felt hopeless as he scanned the surrounding landscape when they stepped back outside onto the church's front steps. Not another building in sight. Just empty farm fields. *Some mission field*, he scolded God silently. How do you grow a church and reach people for Jesus when there aren't any to reach?

Several friendly church members showed up later that month to help Luke move into the parsonage. Invisible hands had filled the kitchen's refrigerator with casseroles, Jell-O salads, and a relish plate. A plastic container of pink-frosted cupcakes rested on the counter, alongside a plate of fresh brownies. As Luke ate the food for his first dinner that night, he forced himself to focus on thoughts for leading the service on Sunday. This would be easy, of course. No need to push himself with heavy, deep-level sermon preparation for a group of thirty retirement-aged people who lived out here in the country. As was becoming his frequent prayer habit, he again reminded God another time that a new, more fitting possibility for him to serve as clergy was needed as soon as such a miracle could open up. "Keep asking…keep seeking…keep knocking…" was already underlined in red in his Bible, and his favorite bookmark had been placed in the book of Matthew so he could return to this scripture quickly. That night before falling asleep, he also wrote that day's date on the page, right next to the verse.

One Sunday morning service seemed to follow another, as the days and then months went by. Between twenty-five and thirty people obediently showed up each week and listened almost without comment to a sermon he typically put together the night before. None of the sermons would have even received better than a C-plus or at most a B-minus back in the days of his seminary homiletics course, he thought often with a twinge of guilt. But why did that matter? This was just fine for these people. Once he got into his next church, however, he'd raise his game with powerful, quality preaching. But right now, what he preached appeared to be enough to satisfy his small congregation. He felt no motivation for anything more.

However, the emptiness and dissatisfaction inside Luke continued to grow. His prayer life and focus on Matthew 7:7 seemed fruitless. One night, three months into his pastorate at Trinity Church, he found himself sleepless, wrestling with the yearning, unfulfilled emptiness that had become his ceaseless companion. He felt so alone. Where was God? What about the sense of call the Holy Spirit had clearly placed on his life back in college, the calling to lead the church of Jesus Christ as a pastor? To see people come to faith, to deepen in spiritual maturity, to serve the needs of others, to grow into a family of faith vibrantly contagious with God's love, like a "city set on a hill" as Jesus had described? But of course, none of that could happen out here.

Well past midnight, Luke unlocked his front door and stepped outside. He found himself walking across the gravel drive and entering the empty, darkened church building. Standing at the altar, he looked up and saw again the colored imagery of a sower sowing seed designed into the stained-glass windows, now lit by moonlight. Then the dam broke inside, and he lay down there on the old hardwood floor, stretched out his arms, and wept. Groanings from his soul, strange utterances of despair echoed from him into the stillness. He cried out to God in his agony to come anew, to fall afresh on his spirit. He began to pray Matthew 7:7 yet again, but this time was different. For the first time, he heard his own words of prayer pleading that God would bring him a new heart, a new mind, and new eyes to feel, perceive, and see how God would bring an answer of any kind to his repeated request.

Luke remained prostrate in the stained-glass moonlight praying for what seemed like hours. When early dawn began to break, he finally arose and sat in the front pew. He felt spent and quiet inside. And surprisingly, an entirely new sense of resolve had emerged. He returned to the parsonage kitchen, and over a cup of coffee, he began to write in his journal.

> I may have only thirty countryside farm folks at the most to hear my sermons each week, but by God's grace I am going to start putting everything I am into preparing and preaching outstanding messages every week—because the excellence of Christ calls me to. Whether I never preach to anyone else other than this little congregation for the rest of my life, I will honor God's call in this way. Every. Single. Sunday.
>
> Also, I am going to begin to get to know each of these people who are my congregation. Even if these couple of dozen persons are the only persons I am ever privileged enough to pastor, I can commit myself to demonstrate Christ's love to them and journey with each of them spiritually, wherever they may be in their faith. And I will do everything I can to inspire them to love and serve their neighbors, even if in this setting they don't really have any close by.
>
> I am going to focus myself on being the pastor—the best pastor possible—of Trinity Church. God, now I wonder if this focus and resolve on behalf of the small congregation you have given me to lead is actually your answer to my Matthew 7:7 prayer! Also, God—this morning, I am realizing that the privilege of serving as Trinity Church's pastor is far more than I really deserve....

The next Sunday, Pastor Luke could hardly wait for the worship service. He had called the pianist a few days before and surprised her by specially requesting two hymns that would align with the theme of his sermon. Only twenty-one people showed up that morning, but they sat attentive and transfixed as Luke delivered what he later noted in his journal as his best sermon ever, woven with spiritual enthusiasm and hope. It was the first of a series, and he announced he would immediately begin a weekly Wednesday night Bible study and prayer gathering to complement it for those who wanted to learn and grow deeper in their faith.

When Luke set up his next sermon series, he announced its theme ahead of time and asked his flock to invite anyone new who might benefit by attending. He was surprised when two members each brought a guest with them to worship, and wondered in passing from where in the nearly deserted miles of fields around the church they might have come. That summer, Luke and the congregation decided to step out beyond the church walls and helped with cleanup at the Maple County Fair, greeting fairgoers as they served. In his morning devotions Luke realized that his Pickaxe Prayer had gradually changed. No longer was he asking God repeatedly for a new church to lead. Instead, he was ceaselessly asking God to continue to transform his congregation, along with himself, into a living example of what Jesus called the body of Christ's believers: a city set on a hill, filled with light.

Only twenty-one months after Luke wrote that first day's date next to Matthew 7:7 in his Bible, weekly attendance at Trinity Church was averaging more than one hundred. The small room used for storage off the sanctuary had had to be cleaned out and renovated by Harry and other members for use as a children's Sunday school and nursery room. Harry and team also erected a simple open-air picnic shelter out behind the church building for a coffee and refreshment time offered during the window of time between the original and the new second worship service that had to be launched in order to accommodate seating. Pastor Luke finally realized that his congregation had networks of friends, colleagues, and family members living widely throughout the area who were now inviting and bringing along to worship. He had never felt more alive, more fulfilled. God was answering his Pickaxe Breakthrough Prayer practice. This was truly a growing, vibrant movement of Jesus happening before their eyes.

Pastor Luke was just walking across the gravel drive to his parsonage after everyone had left church following the second service one Sunday when his cell phone rang. The voice of his district superintendent was on the other end of the line.

"Luke, I well remember how disappointed you were with the assignment to pastor Trinity Church out in Maple County almost two years ago. We have appreciated you swallowing what was a bitter pill and hanging in there. We heard it has gone well. But I have good news!

God must have listened to your prayers. I am calling to let you know that a prime associate pastor position has come open at our largest church in the state, a rare opportunity that would be a significant career move for a young pastor like you. I assume you are interested in getting out of Maple County and back into the city where there are amenities, plus a highly educated, more professional upper-middle class congregation that will appreciate your talents…? This is, of course, what you requested back when you graduated from seminary. We could arrange for you to be reappointed there by the end of the month. Just say the word."

Luke went inside the parsonage and sat down at the kitchen table. There lay his Bible, still opened to the now well-worn page in Matthew where the verse was underlined and dated. He paused, then answered.

"Yes, you are exactly right—God did hear my prayers. I kept asking, then I had to empty myself and be willing to seek so that I could find God's response, and then I had to start knocking on my own hard resistance to a change of my own plans with everything I had. And God did break open new, miraculous possibilities—first in me, and then in the congregation here. I have fallen in love with Trinity Church and Maple County. I am shoulder-to-shoulder with the people I lead and serve. I am living God's answer to my prayers and my calling, right now. You may find this difficult to believe, but I am completely certain of what I'm about to say. I know God wants me to stay and continue right here."

What Can Diminish Pickaxe Prayer?

Back years ago when I listened to the resident woodpecker outside our house, I often wondered how he kept such untiring, relentless zeal for his work. Now, in seasons when I've utilized the Pickaxe Breakthrough Prayer practice in my own leadership journey, it's become evident that certain types of shortfalls can slow or derail me.

Asking, But Not Also "Seeking"

Like Pastor Luke, I keep learning more over time about how to grow in consistent prayer faithfulness, the kind that allows God's Spirit to not only transform the prayer itself but also me as I pray. I have become discouraged at times when my Pickaxe Prayer practice involves a request asking God to break through in a certain situation or need, yet I haven't also augmented the prayer with the guidance from Matthew 7:7 that requires me to seek and do the thoughtful reflection, research, and discernment that might be what's needed for God's transformational response to unfold.

Turbulence or Noisiness of Mind

The ongoing chatter of thoughts happening inside the human mind is capable of creating its own distracting mental commotion that pulls you or me off faith-filled prayer focus and into "what if" imaginings and speculation. As a result, it can become difficult or even impossible to hear, to pick out the calm voice of the Spirit's guidance. And the self-generated commentary of thoughts that are typically driven by worry can become so all-consuming that prayer efforts fall to the wayside. Becoming self-aware when the mental hum of your own thoughts overwhelm the practices of your breakthrough prayer life is central, so that you can intentionally replace them with your Pickaxe Breakthrough Prayers. The extent of the anxious, panicked parade of inner-thought commentary your mind harbors is proportional to your confidence (or lack of it) that God will break through and accomplish what you cannot on your own.

False Discernment

Whenever your Pickaxe Breakthrough Prayer practice is motivated by anger, hurt, resentment, or jealousy of a person or related situation, it's nearly a guarantee that whatever "discernment" you think you have found will merely be expressions of your own punitive attitude and judgment. Surrender to God everything that may be self-serving drivers of your prayer requests, so that your Pickaxe Prayers are personal agenda-less heavenward vessels that carry capacity for God's responsive love to fill and overflow.

God's Silence

Can God trust you with silence? An apparent "God silence" to your Pickaxe Prayer practice is like a spiritual excavating tool, preparing you to receive a response that's something far deeper and greater than you may be asking. Do you really believe that God hears all your prayers, that God is always in process of a response, and that

God's timing can always be trusted? Embracing these truths is the core of that excavation process, chinking away at your own tenacious human desires to control God's answers and outcomes within the timeframe your limited earthly perspective is convinced would be ideal. Impatience with God, however, is a form of unbelief. If God is leading you right now on a Pickaxe Prayer practice journey that is testing your patience and renovating the extent of your willingness to keep praying expectantly, give thanks.

"Impossible" Persons

I have sometimes felt discouraged when continually praying over time for a person who seems far from God and whose convictions (or lack thereof) about spiritual matters or faith remains a door that seems not only closed but tightly locked. Have you? After seeing no evident changes or shifts in the person's behavior or willingness to even discuss the probability of a living and active presence of God in the world, I have felt the threat of futility attempting to dissuade my confidence in God's activity through ongoing Pickaxe Breakthrough Prayer. However, I've learned to consider the plausibility that the Holy Spirit may indeed be slowly working at the subconscious level of that person, where a small crevasse might well exist to allow in slow drops that help supernaturally thaw a long-frozen outlook regarding God's love and invitation.

I invested in a Pickaxe Prayer practice for years on behalf of a family friend who proactively, even sometimes aggressively, attempted to argue the uselessness of the Bible with me every single time we saw each other. Over and over he would proclaim his distaste for all religion from multiple angles and insist God was merely a mytho-logical idea. It felt useless to do so, but I committed myself to keep praying for him even when growing geographical distance caused our in-person encounters to become infrequent over the years. I was astounded during the most recent time I had the opportunity to visit him. There, on the coffee table of his living room, was a Bible, with a bookmark partway through. Even more significant, gone was faith or religion as the very first topic he always brought up, attached to a new argument against. I have confidence in the power of asking, seeking, and knocking—do you?

You—Together with Ministry Traveling Companions

You and your ministry team, council, board, staff, or prayer partners have an unprecedented prospect together to deploy the Pickaxe Breakthrough Prayer practice as a means to open the way for God's new possibilities in your setting. Think now of the current collective prayer life of your team or group when you gather. For what do you pray regularly and consistently, if for anything in particular? Is prayer together mainly for important and immediate prayer concerns or healing that the members of your team name? Is it to ask God's blessing on what you are already doing, or plan to do?

The leadership of the early church of Jesus Christ, as described in the book of Acts, depicts the core nonnegotiable practice of ongoing Pickaxe Prayer together as a privilege and responsibility that opened the way for the Spirit to fuel the contagious movement of believers outward. Beginning in the upper room as noted in Acts 1:14, the initial leaders continually gathered to unite in prayer.

Then, as resistance grew in their surrounding mission field, their leadership Pickaxe Prayer practice became more courageous and direct. As recorded in Acts 4:29-30:

> *Now, Lord, take note of their threats and enable your servants to speak your word with complete confidence. Stretch out your hand to bring healing and enable signs and wonders to be performed through the name of Jesus, your holy servant.* (CEB)

If you are reading this and thinking that your leadership meetings are primarily to take care of business and planning—rather than a future-focused Pickaxe Prayer practice—it may be that your own *ministry activities* have taken the place of persistent prayer requesting *God's activity*. Nothing satiates or neutralizes motivation to pray more reliably than getting busy doing work for God yourselves. While serving the ministry and mission of Jesus is a crucial element for our spiritual growth, a sense of self-sufficiency and self-satisfaction can take over. If we are doing it ourselves, after all, we can control what happens. It is much easier to *do* something ourselves than pray to God. Out of preoccupation with the responsibility of ministry activities can grow spiritual complacency. And out of spiritual complacency proliferates stagnation, then decline.

Jesus taught about Pickaxe Prayer in the face of complacency via a parable about two friends, as recorded in Luke 11:5-10.

> *Then He said to them, "Suppose one of you has a friend, and goes to him at midnight and says to him, 'Friend, lend me three loaves; for a friend of mine has come to me from a journey, and I have nothing to set before him'; and from inside he answers and says, 'Do not bother me; the door has already been shut and my children and I are in bed; I cannot get up and give you anything.' I tell you, even though he will not get up and give him anything because he is his friend, yet because of his persistence he will get up and give him as much as he needs."* (NASB)

The Greek word Jesus used here for "persistence" was also utilized to mean recklessness, audacity, shamelessness, even daring. Is this the characteristic of the Pickaxe Breakthrough Prayer practice of your team or council?

The addition of a diligent Pickaxe Prayer practice—asking, seeking, knocking—could open doors right there in your own setting, where you will find yourselves launched off the dock and riding the rapids of the Spirit together into new adventures, needing to team in different ways, trusting what you cannot yet see up ahead, and hanging on ever more deeply to your faith and trust in the God who is ready to unleash you and your church in new waves of bold fruitfulness. Are you and your team dauntless enough to move beyond your regular duties as council members or staff employees and begin to "knock" on your potential future with Pickaxe Prayers? Even if you find yourselves encountering a resistant surface to such bold prayer—in yourselves?

Pickaxe Prayer Handholds (Prayer-holds)

One of the most beneficial means to help myself incorporate this particular breakthrough prayer practice is the use of a rotating variety of prayer-word handholds, or "prayer-holds." As you've read this chapter, a few of your own Pickaxe Prayer words and phrases may have already sprung to mind. Here are several ideas. Might any of these help you connect more readily and regularly as you ask, seek, and knock?

Continue.

If you tend to pray just once impulsively and do not continually lift a key request to God in such a way that the Spirit might provide transformation and discernment, this prayer-hold could be perfect. Use this one-word prayer to establish a new habit of continuing to cherish your prayers before God. Remember Colossians 4:2, where Paul writes, *"Keep on praying and guard your prayers with thanksgiving"* (CEB). He likewise wrote another early church a reminder to *"pray without ceasing"* (1 Thessalonians 5:17 NASB).

Forward.

Like the athlete pressing onward to win the race and gain the prize, this prayer-hold could assist shifting your focus forward, rather than ruminating on the present challenge (or one in the past) that might have you downcast. Gain inspiration from Philippians 3:13-14: *"I do not regard myself as having laid hold of it yet; but one thing I do: forgetting what lies behind and reaching forward to what lies ahead, I press on toward the goal for the prize of the upward call of God in Christ Jesus"* (NASB).

Endure or Endurance.

This prayer word is like the arrow on a compass, which can point you again and again to the prayer path before you as a reminder to stay the course. *"By your endurance you will gain your lives"* (Luke 21:19 NASB).

Remember.

Paul wrote to his ministry partner Timothy that *"...I constantly remember you in my prayers night and day"* (2 Timothy 1:3 NASB). The use of this prayer word may create in you a new way to think about your Pickaxe Breakthrough Prayers: that by remembering them through each day, you pray them again each time.

Faithful.

A longtime leader in one of my own congregations used to frequently comment, in any and all situations, "God is faithful." At first I wondered if it were simply an unconscious habitual response, just part of conversational exchange with those around her. Later, however, I began to realize it was actually a prayer-hold phrase emanating from her deep, abiding prayer life. She trusted the Almighty to always respond, and this was her way of speaking that affirmation and expectation. *"The one who is calling you is faithful and will do this"* (1 Thessalonians 5:24 CEB).

Discussion or Journal Questions for Application

Keep Asking, Seeking, Knocking is a one-sentence breakthrough prayer practice that becomes useful when you (and/or your team) have, perhaps unintentionally, lapsed into investing your energy primarily in ministry activities and to-do lists, rather than also spiritually positioning yourselves through proactive Pickaxe Prayer to be shaped by God as artists of a potential new future. It's far easier to go through the motions to maintain or tolerate what already is at your church, rather than to persevere with the woodpecker's audacious, doggedness persistence in this collective or individual prayer practice that will change you as well.

Arrange the seating of your group (or if alone, yourself) to face the room's doorway, with the door closed. Open your group discussion or journal time with a minute of silent reflection on what that closed door most symbolically represents to each of you right now in your own life, or in the life of your church.

1. How would you describe the symbolic "closed door" that you just identified? Has the "door" been closed for a long time, or only recently?

Have you attempted to "open" it on your own, or even break through it yourself? If yes, what happened?

2. If you have already prayed about the "closed door" you named, share with the group (or in your journal) what the nature of your prayers have been. For what have you asked God regarding the closed door? Have you asked once, or regularly ongoing?

3. Is there an investment of scripture study, reflection, release of frustration, unforgiveness, or another element that needs to happen for or inside you, to better create inner capacity to listen and hear God's response to your future prayers regarding this? Look back early in this chapter at the expansive meaning of "keep seeking" that Jesus implied in Matthew 7:7. Does anything stand out that you would do well to heed or apply?

4. Consider again your prayer regarding the closed door issue or situation. Is the intention of your prayer request to benefit, please, or protect you? Are there any adjustments to the intention of your prayer that might help you accommodate an expanded latitude within which the Holy Spirit might best accomplish God's goals, rather than your own?

5. Is there any Pickaxe Prayer that the congregation as a whole has been intentionally praying—and if so, around what specifically? Have you observed a response from God that has begun to unfold?

6. This chapter provides several prayer-holds suggestions to augment your Pickaxe Breakthrough Prayer practice. Which of these might be a fit for you? Is there another useful one that comes to mind?

7. Now open the door that's been closed, and keep it open. Allow everyone in the group (or if journaling, just yourself) to reflect on what different feelings might now surface, and how the atmosphere in the room might have changed by opening the door. Let each person share (or journal) whether the opened door seems to pull you forward and invite you to walk through. Or does having the door open seem to violate the intimacy of your group with its unknown beckoning—and invite a sudden threat that someone or something unknown from the "outside" could enter?

8. Pickaxe Prayer that knocks over and over so that the door to the unknown can swing open can also, paradoxically, feel risky and uncontained. What might be on the other side? Discuss whether the cozy comfortability of what *is* might have been, until now, a deterrent to bold prayers to unlock a different outplay.

Concluding Prayer Time

As a group, offer each person a turn that includes the following:

• Pray aloud the "Keep asking, seeking, knocking" Pickaxe Breakthrough Prayer, or a one-word prayer-hold, that you intend to practice as your spiritual discipline for this particular breakthrough prayer practice in the days to come. Name your "take-away" learning about Pickaxe Prayer and what you feel led to implement both as a church leader and in your personal faith walk following Jesus.

• If you wish, identify a Pickaxe Breakthrough Prayer focus for your team, staff, council, or group, and commit together to pray asking, seeking, and knocking. Make sure you revisit it each time you convene, and allow persons to share any insights or breakthroughs they have noticed, or discernment about how the prayer focus should be adjusted or enhanced.

- As each person walks through the open door to leave the room, pause and lay a hand upon the doorframe before you go. Ask God to teach you more and more what it means to "keep knocking" with courage through use of this breakthrough prayer practice.

- Now in your daily living, you can utilize the sight of any open or closed door as a Pickaxe Prayer reminder.

QUICK-REMINDER SUMMARY #5

The fifth bead on my own breakthrough prayer practices strand I described in the introductory "Begin Here" chapter is from **Matthew 7:7**, which I have nicknamed **Pickaxe Prayer: Keep asking, seeking, knocking.**

It's a go-to breakthrough prayer practice of choice when facing a particular challenge, decision, or situation that has no obvious immediate solution to apply or path to take. It's also useful when encountering persons for whom you may feel led to pray spiritually, or who might be harboring anger, a critical heart, difficulty with behavior, or other issues. By asking God with unflagging diligence for your requests, seeking to empty yourself in order to discover and discern, and daring to keep knocking with your prayers against what seems like firm resistance, new breakthroughs are bound to emerge.